IMMERSION
Bible Studies

DEUTERONOMY

D0062715

Praise for IMMERSION

"IMMERSION BIBLE STUDIES is a powerful tool in helping readers to hear God speak through Scripture and to experience a deeper faith as a result."
Adam Hamilton, author of *24 Hours That Changed the World*

"IMMERSION BIBLE STUDIES is a godsend for participants who desire sound Bible study yet feel they do not have large amounts of time for study and preparation. IMMERSION is concise. It is brief but covers the material well and leads participants to apply the Bible to life. IMMERSION is a wonderful resource for today's church."
Larry R. Baird, senior pastor of Trinity Grand Island United Methodist Church

"This beautiful series helps readers become fluent in the words and thoughts of God, for purposes of illumination, strength building, and developing a closer walk with the One who loves us so."
Laurie Beth Jones, author of *Jesus, CEO* and *The Path*

"The IMMERSION BIBLE STUDIES series is no less than a game changer. It ignites the purpose and power of Scripture by showing us how to do more than just know God or love God; it gives us the tools to love like God as well."
Shane Stanford, author of *You Can't Do Everything . . . So Do Something*

"I highly commend to you IMMERSION BIBLE STUDIES, which tells us what the Bible teaches and how to apply it personally."
John Ed Mathison, author of *Treasures of the Transformed Life*

IMMERSION
Bible Studies

DEUTERONOMY

Jack A. Keller, Jr.

Abingdon Press

Nashville

DEUTERONOMY
IMMERSION BIBLE STUDIES
by Jack A. Keller, Jr.

Copyright © 2012 by Abingdon Press

Library of Congress Cataloging-in-Publication Data

Keller, Jack A.
   Deuteronomy / Jack A. Keller, Jr.
      pages cm — (Immersion Bible studies)
   ISBN 978-1-4267-1633-1 (curriculum--printed / text plus-cover : alk. paper) 1. Bible.
O.T. Deuteronomy—Textbooks. I. Title.
   BS1275.55.K45 2012
   222'.150071—dc23

                                                                              2012004881

Editor: Stan Purdum
Leader Guide Writer: Martha Bettis Gee

12 13 14 15 16 17 18 19 20 21—10 9 8 7 6 5 4 3 2 1

Manufactured in the United States of America

Contents

Review Team

Diane Blum
Pastor
East End United Methodist Church
Nashville, Tennessee

Susan Cox
Pastor
McMurry United Methodist Church
Claycomo, Missouri

Margaret Ann Crain
Professor of Christian Education
Garrett-Evangelical Theological Seminary
Evanston, Illinois

Nan Duerling
Curriculum Writer and Editor
Cambridge, Maryland

Paul Escamilla
Pastor and Writer
St. John's United Methodist Church
Austin, Texas

James Hawkins
Pastor and Writer
Smyrna, Delaware

Andrew Johnson
Professor of New Testament
Nazarene Theological Seminary
Kansas City, Missouri

Snehlata Patel
Pastor
Woodrow United Methodist Church
Staten Island, New York

Emerson B. Powery
Professor of New Testament
Messiah College
Grantham, Pennsylvania

Clayton Smith
Pastoral Staff
Church of the Resurrection
Leawood, Kansas

Harold Washington
Professor of Hebrew Bible
Saint Paul School of Theology
Kansas City, Missouri

Carol Wehrheim
Curriculum Writer and Editor
Princeton, New Jersey

IMMERSION BIBLE STUDIES

A fresh new look at the Bible, from beginning to end,
and what it means in your life.

Welcome to IMMERSION!

We've asked some of the leading Bible scholars, teachers, and pastors to help us with a new kind of Bible study. IMMERSION remains true to Scripture but always asks, "Where are you in your life? What do you struggle with? What makes you rejoice?" Then it helps you read the Scriptures to discover their deep, abiding truths. IMMERSION is about God and God's Word, and it is also about you—not just your thoughts, but your feelings and your faith.

In each study you will prayerfully read the Scripture and reflect on it. Then you will engage it in three ways:

Claim Your Story

Through stories and questions, think about your life, with its struggles and joys.

Enter the Bible Story

Explore Scripture and consider what God is saying to you.

Live the Story

Reflect on what you have discovered, and put it into practice in your life.

IMMERSION makes use of an exciting new translation of Scripture, the Common English Bible (CEB). The CEB and IMMERSION BIBLE STUDIES will offer adults:

- the emotional expectation to find the love of God
- the rational expectation to find the knowledge of God
- reliable, genuine, and credible power to transform lives
- clarity of language

Whether you are using the Common English Bible or another translation, IMMERSION BIBLE STUDIES will offer a refreshing plunge into God's Word, your life, and your life with God.

1.

God Is on Your Side!

Deuteronomy 1–4

Claim Your Story

How do you know whether someone is trustworthy? If he or she says, "trust me," do you? If someone asks to borrow a sizeable amount of money and says, "I'll pay you back—honest," do you get out your checkbook? If a salesperson says, "I'm giving you a great deal," do you sign on the dotted line? How far do you trust the people you work with? If you hear, "I'll stick with you through thick and thin," is the speaker a fair-weather or all-weather friend? If someone whispers, "I love you," do you give him or her the key to your heart? If your spouse says, "I won't drink anymore," how confident do you feel that his or her behavior is going to change for the better? If your child insists that he or she is not using illegal drugs, do you feel reassured? If someone says, "I'm doing the best I can," do you cut him or her a little slack? If you hear, "I'm sorry," can you ever trust that person again?

Most of us are cautious about letting down our guard when we first meet someone, regardless of what that person says or promises. Trust grows incrementally as we develop a relationship and a "track record" with others. If we see evidence that someone can be trusted, we normally venture more. At some point, we see enough evidence that we stop looking for evidence and simply assume that promises will be kept, that a person can be trusted with the tender places in our lives. Until a promise is broken. Until we are wounded. And then, if the damage is not too great and the chasm not too wide, the process starts over again. We watch carefully to see if someone has changed enough in a positive way to be worthy of our trust.

In short, we decide whom to trust and how much to trust by observing past behavior. If someone consistently does what he or she promises to do, we learn to expect that and to count on it. If someone is consistently in our corner, we have reason to believe she will be there in the future. If someone consistently acts as if he has our best interest at heart, we tend to believe he will act that way tomorrow and next year and the year after that.

Do you trust God? Maybe a better question would be, "How much do you trust God?" What evidence do you have that God is trustworthy? Looking back over your life, when and where have you seen or felt God at work? What evidence has there been to suggest that God is on your side? Do you have good reason to trust that God will continue to be on your side?

That was the crux of the matter for ancient Israel. In this opening chapter, we'll take a closer look at that, along with some other matters important to the writer of the Book of Deuteronomy.

Enter the Bible Story

The name of the fifth book of the Bible provides two clues to what the book is about. The Hebrew title is taken from the opening words: "These are the words." More than the four preceding books in the Torah/ Pentateuch and more than the historical books that follow, Deuteronomy is a book of crucial words. It consists almost entirely of the words of Moses, but Moses often conveys the words of the Lord.

The name of this book familiar to English readers, *Deuteronomy*— meaning "the second law" or a "copy of the law"—is taken from the Greek translation of Deuteronomy 17:18. The book is a collection of law and teaching that builds on the first law, the Ten Commandments given at Mount Sinai (or, as Deuteronomy prefers to call it, Mount Horeb).

The Theology of the Land

The land, says Deuteronomy repeatedly, is a gift from God to Israel. In fifteen explicit references, Deuteronomy tells us the land was promised to the patriarchs as a gift. A promise to our ancestors, says Deuteronomy to the people of his time, is a promise to us.

But the promise requires a response. God has given the land but the Israelites are told many times that they must go into the land and possess it (Deuteronomy 3:18; 4:1, 5, 14; 6:18; 8:1; 9:1; 11:8, 10-11; 30:16). God is in charge completely, according to Deuteronomy, but the people have to participate in what God is doing.

The Promised Land is filled with abundance (Deuteronomy 1:25, 35; 3:25; 4:21, 22; 6:18; 8:7-10; 9:6; 11:17), "full of milk and honey" (6:3; 11:9; 26:9,15; 27:3; 31:20). It offers all that is necessary for a life of prosperity. The land even comes with God's provision of cities, houses, cisterns, vineyards, and olive trees (6:10-11). The land is a place to rest after the weariness of wandering, a place of peace for a people plagued by enemies and conflict, a place to live comfortably in covenant with God.

About the Christian Faith

The Forgotten Form of Sin

The word *sloth* doesn't slither across my breakfast table very often. How about you? Does the word conjure up *National Geographic* photos of a slow-moving animal that hangs from trees in South American tropical forests? Or perhaps you think of it simply as a synonym for laziness. In Christian tradition, however, *sloth* is an important theological term. It refers to one of the two principal forms of sin.

Throughout the history of Christian teachings, the dominant strand has understood sin as an expression of excessive *pride*. Sin as pride means self-assertion run amuck, thinking too highly of ourselves, trying to take the place of God. But there has also been a subdominant theme of sin as *sloth*. If pride is thinking too highly of ourselves, sloth is thinking less of ourselves than we should. Sloth is the antithesis of the US Army slogan, "Be all you can be!" When we succumb to sloth, we are not being and doing all that we could and should. We are *under*estimating ourselves. When fear and anxiety about the future paralyze us, even when there are good reasons for confidence and hope, we are in the grip of sin as sloth.

Such was the case with the Exodus generation of Israel that refused to unwrap the package when the gift of the land was offered. God's record of saving actions in the past provided ample grounds for trusting God in the future. But the "descendants of the Anakites" (Deuteronomy 1:28; NRSV, "Anakim"), mighty and tall, struck fear in the hearts of the Israelites and they doubted God's will or ability to protect and sustain them. They hesitated, which actually meant they went backward instead of moving forward.

But rest and peace and comfort are contingent, according to Deuteronomy, upon Israel's response to a generous God. Israel will flourish if it loves and obeys the Lord; but the land will be lost if Israel does not. There could be no more terrible punishment.

The land is closely related to the law. As Moses announces in Deuteronomy 12:1, "These are the regulations and the case laws that you must carefully keep in the fertile land the LORD, your ancestors' God, has given to you to possess for as long as you live on that land" (NRSV, "all the days that you live on the earth"). Many of the regulations and case laws in Deuteronomy are explicitly associated with the land and Israel's life in it. Obedience is not simply a matter of doing whatever it takes to avoid divine retribution. Rather, the commandments are a necessity for both (1) a right relationship with God; and (2) a healthy, harmonious community. The commandments are guidelines for living happily in community under God.

Christians properly think of the land not as geographically specific but as the place—any place—where God has put us. Our use of land and property affects our neighbors and our posterity and so has theological and moral importance. We understand the Deuteronomic claim that home, family, work and the rewards it brings, all are desirable and part of God's intention. But we sometimes forget Deuteronomy's insistence that ultimately the land and all that it represents comes to us as a divine gift, not by legal right, not by family inheritance, not from our physical labor and mental exertion. We participate in what God is doing; we don't do it by ourselves. Whatever we have, we use at the pleasure of the Lord who owns it all.

The Four "Israels" of Deuteronomy

A careful reader will discover that there are four different "Israels" in the Book of Deuteronomy. One Israel mentioned in Deuteronomy is the *first generation* of Hebrews who crossed the Red Sea and received the Ten Commandments at Mount Sinai. This is the generation that balked at the prospect of actually entering the Promised Land and consequently wandered in the wilderness for the rest of their lives. Another Israel in Deuteronomy's story is the generation to which Moses was ostensibly speaking just east of the Jordan River. This Israel is the *second generation* of the Hebrews who fled from Egypt, which is no longer wandering in the wilderness but is poised to enter the land of Canaan. Yet a *third* Israel is the audience(s) that the writers of Deuteronomy addressed in their own time, which likely spanned the eighth to sixth centuries B.C. This third Israel lived long, long after the Exodus generation and the generation on the boundary between the wilderness and the land of milk and honey. This third Israel was the Southern Kingdom of Judah during its last one hundred to two hundred years as an independent nation *and* after Judah fell to the Babylonians and the people were dragged off into exile.

Deuteronomy presumes a profound continuity across all three Israels. The promises to the Patriarchs are promises to every Israel. The story of liberation from Egypt and receiving the gift of the law is the story of "all Israel" across generations and centuries. Trusting and doubting God in the wilderness and alternately obeying and disobeying God is the pattern repeated in every "Israel." Even after the land is claimed and settled, the pattern continues. The norm, the standard of expectation, is loving God and doing justice. The reality repeatedly falls short—eventually with very serious consequences. So for Deuteronomy the basic message to all three "Israels" is the same: Trust and obey the Lord.

Contemporary believers comprise the *fourth* "Israel." *We* are the "you" to whom God speaks through Moses and the biblical record. We are the ones alternately fearful and faithful. We are the ones who vacillate between joyful obedience and stubborn rebellion. So the basic message of Deuteronomy applies to us as well: Trust and obey God.

Qualifications of Leaders

Moses needs help. The demands of leadership are too heavy for him to bear alone. Deuteronomy 1:9-18 reiterates what appeared earlier in Exodus 18:13-23 and Numbers 11:14-17. Those individuals who would function as judges should be "wise, discerning, and well-regarded" (Deuteronomy 1:13).

Moses gives them four basic instructions. First, they are to "judge fairly" (1:16, CEB and NIV; NRSV, "judge rightly"). Second, judges are not to show partiality but are to "hear both small and great alike" (Deuteronomy 1:17a, NIV). The "small" are the weak and the poor, the supposedly unimportant. The "great" are the rich and powerful, who think of themselves as important and are regarded that way by many.

Third, those charged with administering justice must not be susceptible to intimidation by anyone; otherwise, justice is compromised (Deuteronomy 1:17b). This particular danger is as real today as it was when Moses spoke and when Deuteronomy was written. Remember the financial crisis of the late 2000s, which plunged the United States into the worst recession since the Great Depression of the 1930s. It was not a natural disaster, but a consequence of greed on Wall Street and elsewhere. Millions of ordinary citizens paid a hefty price for that fiasco. But how many elite business leaders who engineered the financial disaster en route to enormous corporate and personal gain have been brought to justice in either criminal or civil courts? Petty thieves are easy to bring to justice; not so, movers and shakers. No wonder Martin Luther said of the need for leaders to avoid intimidation, "This is the highest and most difficult virtue of rulers, namely, justice and integrity of judgment. For it is easy to pronounce judgment on poor and common people; but to condemn the powerful, the wealthy, and the friendly, to disregard blood, honor, fear, favor, and gain and simply to consider the issue—this is a divine virtue."[1]

Finally, when matters are too complicated for a judge to handle, Moses is available as a kind of Supreme Court that renders justice (Deuteronomy 1:17c).

Israel's Initial Refusal to Enter the Land

When the people of Israel are first told that the land is theirs for the taking, they suffer a collective case of the jitters. They think the good news is too good to be true—and they head back toward the Red Sea.

Almost hidden in this rehearsal of doubt and disobedience (Deuteronomy 1:19-46) is a little gem, a juxtaposition of two images of God. Moses tries to reassure the Israelites by speaking of the Lord as both *warrior* and *parent*. "The LORD your God . . . will fight for you" (1:30). Throughout the entire journey "the LORD your God has carried you just as a parent carries a child" (1:31).

The Exodus generation was not reassured. But some among later generations *were* reassured, as we are, at least when focusing on this twofold picture of God. God stretches over us a mighty arm, like a warrior, and a tender protecting arm, like a parent. Whatever threatening situation we may face, as individuals or as a community, God is with us, watching over us, and working ("fighting") for our well-being. Come what may, God cares about us, supports us, and, so far as we will allow, guides and nurtures us.

God Is on Your Side

Israel positioned at the boundary between the wilderness and the new land was only one nation among many—and a puny one at that. Not sharing Israel's privileged understanding of God, those other nations were intimidating. So Moses reminds Israel of God's mighty acts of salvation on its behalf. He begins at the beginning. The Lord whom Israel worships is the creator of all human beings, whether they know it or not. "Has anything this amazing ever happened? Has anything like it ever been heard of

Across the Testaments

We Respond to What God Has Already Done

Deuteronomy 4:1 begins, "Now, Israel, in light of all that [God had done since Israel left Mount Horeb], listen to the regulations and the case laws that I am teaching you to follow. . . ." Those who have been the beneficiaries of God's grace are called to live in trust and obedience.

We see a similar pattern in the New Testament in Paul's use of "therefore" or "so [then]" at:

Romans 12:1—"So, brothers and sisters, because of God's mercies, I encourage you to present your bodies as a living sacrifice that is holy and pleasing to God."

Ephesians 4:1—"Therefore, as a prisoner for the Lord, I encourage you to live as people worthy of the call you received from God."

Ephesians 5:1-2—"Therefore, imitate God like dearly loved children. Live your life with love, following the example of Christ, who loved us and gave himself for us."

Philippians 2:12-13, where immediately after Paul presents the story of Christ's incarnation as the model for humility and obedience, Paul writes, "Therefore, my beloved, . . . work out your own salvation with fear and trembling; for it is God who is at work in you" (NRSV).

Because of the good news that we are loved by God, we are called to live in a manner consistent with the gospel.

before?" (4:32). Not only is God the Creator, but God has spoken to them from fire. God liberated the Hebrew slaves from Egypt with "tests, miracles, wonders, war" and "awesome power" (4:33-34). The Lord has established a covenant with Israel, providing both a place to live and instruction about how to flourish as a community. All of this has demonstrated that God loves the people of Israel and can be trusted to care for them. They have good reasons to trust God and to do their part to honor the covenant.

Live the Story

What would it take to persuade you that God is on your side—not *only* yours, but *truly* yours? Do you claim for yourself, as the Christian church claims, the legacy of the people of Israel: freedom *from* bondage and freedom *for* a covenantal relationship with the Lord God?

Do the mighty acts of God in the New Testament persuade you that God cares deeply about you? After all, has the Creator of heaven and earth, the King of the universe, ever stooped so low to enter the world as a helpless baby? Has any people ever seen and heard as clearly what God is like as you have in Christ Jesus? Has any people known a Savior who loved us enough to die for us while we were still sinners? Has any people ever been baptized by water and the Spirit of God? Has any people ever been invited to the table of the Lord? Has any people ever been made a new creation? What more would it take to persuade you?

1. From Luther's *Lectures on Deuteronomy*, quoted in Patrick D. Miller, *Deuteronomy*. Interpretation (Louisville: John Knox, 1990), 30.

2.
A Relationship
and a Way of Living

Deuteronomy 5:1–6:19

Claim Your Story

In recent years, "smartphones" have taken the telephone market by storm. They have tremendous customer appeal. Each new model makes it easier to access everything that can be converted to digital format. People don't merely talk and text with their phones; they carry their offices and their entertainment with them. Hundreds of "apps" make it possible to hold the world in the palm of one's hand.

The level of enthusiasm for this particular technology was captured in an iconic photo, beamed around the world, of four young men with smiles on their faces who were waiting outside a store on launch day for the latest and best smartphone. Each of the young men was wearing a black band around his head. Attached to the band in the center of his forehead was a full-color, full-size mock-up of the new phone. It was obvious, to say the least, that this new gizmo represented something very important to all four.

If you were going to announce what you care about most by wearing a symbol of it on your forehead, what would it be? Would you wear the same symbol every day and everywhere you went? Or would you need a different symbol at work, at home, at church, and at the ball game?

Deuteronomy 5–6 tells about what ancient Israelites wore to remind themselves and to announce to others what is most important. At the top of that pyramid of value, says Deuteronomy, is a relationship and a way of living. The bedrock of that relationship and that way of life is found in the Ten Commandments and the *Shema*.

Enter the Bible Story

The Ten Commandments

The prologue to the Ten Commandments in Deuteronomy 5:6 reminds us that the people who are given the commandments are *already* God's people. The law is not a means of salvation; rather, the law is instruction about how persons who are already loved by God should live. God's love precedes God's demands.

The **first commandment**, "You must have no other gods before me" (5:7), has multiple meanings. The basic meaning, applicable to the age in which the commandments were first given, was to prohibit the worship of any deity except the Lord. The common assumption in that time was that other gods exist. This commandment, however, declares that Israel was not to worship them. No deity is to be given priority over the Lord in terms of worship and obedience.

Another possible meaning is "You shall have no other gods over against me." That is, the Israelites were not to worship or obey gods in hostile conflict with the Lord. The story of Elijah's contest with the Canaanite deity Baal (see 1 Kings 18) is illustrative. The Lord and Baal are rival deities and the people of Israel have to choose between them. Deuteronomy 5:7 can also be read as "You must have no gods in addition to me, in preference to me, or in place of me." The kernel of meaning here is that there simply *is* no deity anywhere besides the Lord. Israel's God is also Lord of everything! There is only one God of the universe, to whom all nature and all nations and all people are subject.

The common ground shared by these several interpretations of verse 7 is the conviction that a relationship of worship, loyalty, and trust is appropriate only with the Lord. One nuance of meaning or another may have carried more weight at different times in Israel's history.

Interpretations of the **second commandment** (5:8-10) fall into two broad categories. One interpretation reads the commandment as prohibiting the making or worshiping of physical representations of other gods *besides* the Lord. But many scholars favor a different interpretation, concluding that this commandment prohibits making or worshiping of a physical representation *of* the Lord. Why the prohibition against making images of God?

We can identify four plausible lines of reasoning. First, no created object can possibly do justice to God's transcendence, mystery, beauty, and glory. All images of God are inadequate, whether made of wood, stone, metal, or paint on canvas. The true God always transcends our grasp.

A second possible reason for this commandment is that it underscores God's *relatedness*. Physical representations of a deity are static, unable to act or move, unable to hear or speak, without thought or feeling. But Israel's God *does* think, feel, hear, speak, and act. Israel's God *does* care about human beings.

A third plausible reason for the prohibition against images of God may be that it serves to guard against the impulse to try to control God. The close association between a worshiper and an image of a deity may lead to a false notion that the worshiper has control of the deity and can manipulate its power for the worshiper's own ends. As Old Testament scholar Ronald Clements has put it, "the most terrible blasphemy is to believe that God can be kept 'in one's pocket.'"[1]

A fourth plausible reason points back to Genesis 1:26-27, which says that God created human beings in the divine image and likeness. Perhaps only human beings—flawed and finite as we are—can represent God in the created world.

Deuteronomy 5:9, which in the New Revised Standard Version (NRSV), New International Version (NIV), and some other translations describes God as "jealous," may trouble you. We don't normally think of jealousy as a virtue; in fact, we see too much evidence that unhealthy jealousy can be destructive. Poet and author Kathleen Norris offers an insightful counterbalance: "The word 'jealousy' has its roots in 'zealous,' denoting extreme enthusiasm and devotion, and God's jealousy retains the word's more positive aspects. It helps us to trust. Who, after all, would trust a

God, a parent, spouse, lover, who said to us, 'I really love you, but I don't care at all what you do or who you become?'"[2] The Common English Bible (CEB) translation says that God is "passionate"; that is, God cares deeply about Israel (and by extension, about *us*).

Much more is at stake in the **third commandment** (5:11) about the use of God's name than cursing and foul speech. The core idea is that God's name should not be used emptily, trivially, cheaply, for no good purpose, and certainly not for any morally worthless or evil purpose.

This commandment rules out a number of behaviors. We are not to treat God's name lightly. We are not to use God's name for personal profit or for political advantage. This commandment, if taken seriously, would rule out politicians invoking God's name in campaign speeches in order to win votes; public officials equating God with country to justify morally questionable military action; televangelists using God's name in shameless appeals for money; and, closer to home, parents who present a child for baptism and then never show up in church again. The list could go on and on. God is not to be used as a means toward one of our self-centered ends. Praise and prayer are the appropriate postures for speaking the name of God, always lifting up God's name for honor.

In the **fourth commandment** (5:12-15), the sabbath is set apart, first and foremost, for rest from work. *Everyone* is to rest from their labors: the rich and the poor, masters and servants, parents and children, resident foreigners, and even domesticated animals. Why? Deuteronomy 5:12-15 says that the sabbath is to help the people remember that God delivered Israel from unceasing hard labor in Egypt. The version of this commandment in Exodus 20:8-11 says that sabbath observance is in imitation of God resting on the seventh day of Creation. With either supporting rationale, one implication of this commandment is clear: We are more, in God's eyes, than the work we do for a living. We have value, quite apart from our achievements, because of our relationship with God.

The **fifth commandment** (5:16) is addressed primarily to adult children with elderly parents. Members of the older generation are not to be thrown aside when their productive years have passed. Once again, the implication is that our worth does not come exclusively from our current level of productivity. Aged parents deserve respect and loving care as full members of their families and their communities. By implication, the mandate to honor parents extends to honoring all the members of the elderly generation, whether blood kin or not.

About the Scripture

Phylacteries and Mezuzahs

Phylacteries are small boxes, made from the leather of kosher animals, boxes that contain specific scriptural passages and are fastened to the forehead and arm with leather thongs. Each box contains four biblical passages: Exodus 3:1-10; 13:11-16; Deuteronomy 6:4-9; 11:13-21. Though the word *phylacteries* comes from a Greek word meaning "amulet," they were not in any way connected with magic. Rather, they are reminders of the Torah and Israel's special relationship with God.

While phylacteries were intended as a sign of genuine piety, Matthew 23:5 reports Jesus sharply criticizing hypocritical Pharisees who wear phylacteries for show.

Like phylacteries, *mezuzahs* were a way of marking oneself as remembering the commands of the covenant. A mezuzah was a small container, attached to the doorpost of a home, that held a copy of Deuteronomy 6:4-9 and 11:13-21.

The central interpretive issue with the **sixth commandment** (5:17) is how far-reaching the prohibition against taking human life should be understood. The CEB translates the verse as "Do not kill" (with "do not murder" in a footnote as the alternative translation). The NRSV says "You shall not murder" (with "you shall not kill" as a footnoted translation). Support for "murder" can be found in the fact that the Hebrew verb used is not one of the general words for killing. Generally, the verb refers to homicide, a deliberate taking of life. But there are exceptions, when the verb also refers to manslaughter. In any case, the basic point is clear: All life belongs to God. One is not, under ordinary circumstances, to usurp God's ownership by taking the life of one's neighbor. Put positively, this commandment obliges us to do whatever is necessary to protect the life of the neighbor.

In its original patriarchal context, the **seventh commandment** (5:18) prohibited sexual relations between a man, regardless of whether he was married or not, and a married woman. Clearly, there was a double standard!

We don't, as modern readers, have to endorse that double standard to recognize and claim something terribly important in this commandment. Sexuality is not meant to be a casual matter. Marital relationships are important—and fragile. Women as well as men need to be perceived as persons of worth and deserving of profound respect. Trust only grows in a secure environment. Families are crucially important—and flourish best when characterized by the bedrock of a solid and lasting bond between the parents.

Put positively, this commandment calls us to love our neighbor by protecting and honoring the neighbor's marriage and family. In so doing, one's own marriage and family will be protected.

The verb *steal* in the **eighth commandment** (5:19) has no object. Stealing *anything* is prohibited. Stealing can be defined as both (1) taking from people anything that rightfully belongs to them, and (2) taking from people whatever they are entitled to receive.

Property and possessions are to some degree an extension of the person who is the owner. So stealing from someone is a violation of that person. One can readily understand why, in a predominantly poor population, theft would be a serious problem. The theft of a cloak, a donkey or ox, or a crucial tool would have been catastrophic for a poor person. Even for persons who are comparatively well off, theft feels like a personal violation, as any victim of a burglary knows firsthand.

Stealing applies to a wide range of behaviors that are all too common in today's world. Fraudulent financial advisors are stealing. Employers who fail to provide fair pay and fair benefits are stealing. Workers who fail to provide a day's work for a day's pay are stealing. Power brokers who make policy decisions that benefit a few while depriving many of community resources are stealing. Individual and corporate consumers who use disproportionate amounts of scarce natural resources and generate excessive levels of pollution are stealing from future generations. This commandment seems like such a simple rule; but taken as a core principle, it has far-reaching implications.

The **ninth commandment** (5:20) is aimed primarily at preventing false witness in the judicial process. Justice in courts depends upon truthful testimony. False testimony, in ancient Israel as in today's society, can have terrible consequences.

This commandment came to include a broader meaning as well. Lying about a neighbor in gossip or slander is prohibited (see Leviticus 19:16; Hosea 4:2). Making any false statement that would harm another person's reputation is forbidden. Put positively, we are to be truthful in all settings, using speech to edify others rather than to diminish or destroy them.

The **tenth commandment** (5:21), not to covet anything that belongs to one's neighbor, suggests that obedience is a matter of heart and mind, of intentions and attitudes. Recognizing that covetousness breeds discontent, this commandment calls for restraint of inordinate desire.

Obedience to this commandment is perhaps especially challenging for those of us immersed in a culture that encourages coveting (endlessly wanting more and more) as the engine for a robust economy. "Enough" is what most of us would be glad to have if we didn't see our neighbors with more. But we seem to have a predisposition to see whatever our neighbor has as the measure of our own satisfaction. The problem is magnified by relentless advertising that portrays the good life as an existence of endless consumption.

The Shema

Deuteronomy 6:4-9, which begins with the Hebrew word *shema* (shee-MAH, "Hear"), is a central confession of faith not only for ancient Israel but also for later Judaism and Christianity. It provides a sense of who God is, who the listeners or readers are as a people, and the nature of the relationship between God and the people.

A careful look at any of the leading English translations of Deuteronomy 6:4 (see, for instance, CEB, NIV, or NRSV) provides a hint of the complexity of this verse. The first half of the verse proclaims that

---

Across the Testaments

The Great Commandment

The Great Commandment of Deuteronomy 6:4-5 is echoed in the Gospels where Jesus quotes it as the "first" and greatest of the commandments (Matthew 22:34-40; Mark 12:28-34; Luke 10:25-38). The Markan passage is distinctive in two respects. First, it includes the first part of Deuteronomy 6:4 ("Hear, O Israel . . ."). Second, the Markan passage confirms the double meaning of Deuteronomy 6:4: (1) the Lord is one, and (2) besides the Lord there is no other (see Mark 12:32).

"our God is the LORD." The second half of the verse uses a Hebrew expression that is ambiguous; it can be understood either as "the LORD alone" or "the LORD is one." So which is it? The two meanings are not the same. Both can be supported by plausible arguments and evidence. Probably the best course is to assume that the writers of Deuteronomy recognized the ambiguity and intended the fullness of the double meaning.

What is the import of the pronouncement that God is one? It means that the Lord is neither divided nor capricious. The One worthy of trust and worship is consistent in character and purpose. There is no incongruity between the presence and activity of God *here* and *now* and the presence and activity of God *there* and *then*. Deuteronomy is telling the ancient Israelites (and us) that there is no reason to think that sometimes God is *for* us and sometimes *against* us or sometimes *caring* and sometimes *indifferent*.

The other possible translation of Deuteronomy 6:4 is "The LORD is our God, the LORD alone" (NRSV; CEB, "Our God is the LORD! Only the LORD!"). The spiritual and psychological insight beneath this affirmation is that *freedom from* is always linked to *freedom for*. Serving some god or other is an inescapable part of the human condition. The real issue is, *which* God will be served? Deuteronomy is asking, to whom will Israel be loyal? Where will the people of God place their ultimate loyalty?

While Deuteronomy 4:39 denies that there are other gods ("the LORD is the only God in heaven above and on earth below"), Deuteronomy 6:4

doesn't insist on the existence of only one God, but that for *you* (the Israelites and us) there is only one God, only One due ultimate allegiance. There may be other claims upon your loyalty, but none shall be at the same level as the claim of the Lord God. The ancient Israelites struggled with the temptation to hedge their bets by worshiping lesser gods and goddesses alongside the Lord.

We Christians struggle with a similar temptation, don't we? At one level, we want to worship and serve the one true God. But at a functional level, we build our lives around other values and other powers (money, success, status, family, addiction, country, and more) right alongside or even instead of God.

Two aspects of the Great Commandment (6:5) are especially noteworthy. First, the Israelites are *commanded* to *love* God. We contemporary Western readers may find that odd. So acclimated to a popular culture that assumes love is an emotion, ofttimes a romantic feeling, we wonder, "How can affection be commanded?" But Deuteronomy does not reduce love to an emotion. Not unconnected to a sense of awe and reverence before God, this love finds expression in loyalty and service. We demonstrate our love by living the way God wants us to live—that is, staying in a close relationship to God, keeping the commandments, and, as the prophet Micah puts it, walking humbly with our God (Micah 6:8).

The second aspect of the Great Commandment that deserves special mention is that it calls for *total* commitment. We are to love God with everything we've got, with our whole self, with our entire devotion. We are not to restrict God to one compartment of our lives, but to love God with our whole being.

Some may wonder, "Does that mean I can't love anything else?" No, Deuteronomy is not forbidding its readers to love anything else; after all, many lesser loves (family, vocation, country, church, and more) are healthy, even necessary. What Deuteronomy is saying is that secondary interests and loyalties are just that: secondary. Only one center of value can be primary in our lives: the Lord God.

(For discussion of Deuteronomy 6:20-25, see Session 5.)

Live the Story

It's not always easy to get our priorities straight. It's not always easy to live them out even after we know what they should be. What's most important in *your* life? Does your relationship with God have priority over other relationships? What functional difference does that make? What basic principles are guiding your actions? What kind of person are those principles shaping you to be?

1. Ronald E. Clements, "The Book of Deuteronomy: Introduction, Commentary, and Reflections," in Volume 2 of *The New Interpreter's Bible*, edited by Leander E. Keck (Nashville: Abingdon, 1998), 321.
2. Norris, *Amazing Grace: A Vocabulary of Faith* (New York: Riverhead Books, 1998), 87.

3.

Remembering
the Lord's Provision

Deuteronomy 7–11

Claim Your Story

If you're a Civil War-history enthusiast or an old-movie buff, you may remember the 1965 movie starring Jimmy Stewart titled *Shenandoah*. Set in 1863, the movie tells the story of a wealthy Virginian, Charlie Anderson (Stewart), who works his ranch in the heart of the Shenandoah Valley with his six sons and one daughter (and without any slaves). Anderson tries to keep his family separated and safe from the Civil War raging around them—to no avail. The movie was popular on both sides of the Mason-Dixon Line and contains several memorable scenes.

Anderson is a crusty, autocratic character without any interest in religion. But his wife was a fervent Christian and her final wish before her death was that her husband would raise their children to be good Christians. So when the family gathers around a table filled with the bounty of the land, Anderson offers this perfunctory prayer of thanksgiving: "Lord, we cleared this land. We plowed it, sowed it, and harvested it. We cooked the harvest. It wouldn't be here and we wouldn't be eating it if we hadn't done it all ourselves. We worked dog-bone hard for every crumb and morsel, but we thank you Lord just the same for the food we're about to eat. Amen."

We laugh at the audacity of Anderson's attitude. After all, who made the fertile soil that he cultivates? Whence the rain that waters his crops? Who blessed him with six strapping sons and a beautiful daughter? Where did he get the knowledge and good health that allows him to make the land productive?

But perhaps some of us have harbored thoughts similar to those of Charlie Anderson, though we may be careful not to say them aloud for fear of censure. When we have worked hard for years, delaying gratification for a greater reward later, don't we like to think that we deserve the benefits we enjoy? Don't those of us who are comfortably well-off prefer to think that our success is due largely to our own efforts?

You may not identify with Charlie Anderson. Your situation may not be analogous to that of a wealthy rancher but more like a sharecropper trying to scratch out a living on land he or she doesn't own. If so, when you read the Book of Deuteronomy, you may identify more closely with the generation of Israelites who had endured a tough life in the wilderness and who waited expectantly for a better life in the Promised Land. Moses' speeches are directed to that generation of Israelites, offering hope and comfort to the afflicted.

Perhaps, on the other hand, you *can* imagine yourself in the shoes of Charlie Anderson—with all the necessary updates for the twenty-first century. Deuteronomy is speaking to you, too, in the warnings to Israelites of a later generation who are prosperous and comfortable in the land. Their material contentment, Deuteronomy fears, has led to spiritual atrophy. Their self-confidence has become hubris. What they need to hear is a message that afflicts the comfortable. We'll take a closer look at this when we examine Deuteronomy 8 in particular.

Enter the Bible Story

The Election of Israel

Chapter 7 of Deuteronomy strikes many contemporary readers as morally problematic. We may be comfortable with Moses telling the Israelites that "you are a people holy to the LORD your God. The LORD your God chose you to be his own treasured people beyond all others on the fertile land" (7:6). But we squirm at the notion that God is complicit in Israel's utter destruction of the peoples already in the land (7:1-5).

Of course, if we are honest about our own national history, we realize that America has not always been morally fastidious about such things. Our forefathers and foremothers embraced the doctrine of "manifest destiny," presuming divine sanction for the territorial expansion of the United States. Convinced of the rightness of our cause, our treatment of native peoples during the nineteenth and twentieth centuries was often duplicitous and sometimes brutal. Perhaps every country that has opportunity to expand its territory or its empire finds ways to justify its actions.

About the Scripture

The Scope of God's Blessing

The command in Deuteronomy 7 to destroy utterly seven nations in order to possess the land is preceded by the report in 2:24–3:7 of the annihilation of the areas east of the Jordan River. But Moses forbids the Israelites to attack three peoples who are distant relatives (2:3-19). The Edomites are descendants of Esau, the brother of Jacob, and the Moabites and Ammonites are kindred of Lot, the nephew of Abraham. God has already given these peoples their land as a possession (2:5, 9, 19).

This raises an interesting idea: God's blessing, demonstrated in the gift of the land, is not exclusive to a single people. The scope of divine love is wider than just Israel, wider than just "us."

But back to ancient Israel. What do we make of the violence that accompanies Israel's election by God? First, we should recognize that Moses pulls the rug out from under any claim that Israel *deserves* special treatment from God. Israel is not favored because it is bigger than other nations (7:7). Neither is Israel chosen because of its virtue. The nations that the Lord promises to displace are declared wicked; but Israel is not being given their land because the Israelites are particularly righteous or Israel's heart is especially virtuous (see 9:4-5). God chooses Israel for two reasons, neither of which entails merit: "[I]t is because the LORD loved you and because he kept the solemn pledge he swore to your ancestors" (7:8). God's choosing of Israel is sheer grace!

Second, while a literal reading of Deuteronomy would strike most contemporary readers as morally troubling, we need to remember that Deuteronomy was written long after the people of Israel moved into the Promised Land. The writer knew that Israel did not in fact strictly carry out Moses' orders for the conquest. We see evidence in other Old Testament books that Israel did not slaughter entire populations. The children of Israel did marry Canaanites. And the gods of the Canaanites persisted as a powerful temptation for the Israelites for centuries. In short, the writer of Deuteronomy was aware of Israel's long history of compromise with pagan religious and cultural values, all the way from the entrance into Canaan to the fall of Judah. Deuteronomy says in the clearest possible terms that those compromises were terrible mistakes, poisoning Israel's covenantal relationship with the Lord—but the historical record is not as bloody as the rhetoric.

We still have to wonder, though, what we can affirm in these texts. If we cannot embrace the extreme violence of Chapter 7, is there still a message here that we *can* claim? I think there is.

At the heart of the covenantal relationship between the Lord and the people is the expectation that Israel's response to God should mirror God's relationship to Israel. The Lord loves Israel and is faithful to the divine promises. God expects the people of Israel to love wholeheartedly in return and to live according to the commandments. God is holy and expects God's chosen people to be holy, too.

Being "holy to the LORD" means to be set apart for a special purpose, to be separate in some respects, to be special, distinctive. Israel had a special mission as the chosen people: to be instruments of God's blessing for the entire world. Abram (later called Abraham) is told "all the families of earth will be blessed because of you" (Genesis 12:3). Isaiah 42:6 and 49:6 declare that God's servant, Israel, will be "a light to the nations." The covenant community is to be "the showcase of divine love and justice."[1]

To be true to that mission, Israel could not be just like the other peoples. To be faithful, Israel had to be different. Deuteronomy holds nothing back in rejecting idolatry. Even a whiff of idolatry is a threat that must be eliminated at all costs—even extermination of the idolaters.

A Holy Nation, God's Own People in the New Testament

Continuing in the covenant tradition, 1 Peter 2:9 declares that the Christian community is "a chosen race, a royal priesthood, a holy nation, God's own people" (NRSV). Is this a matter of privilege or merit? No. "You have become this people so that you may speak of the wonderful acts of the one who called you out of darkness into his amazing light" (CEB). We, too, have a mission: proclaiming in word and deed and lifestyle the redeeming love of God revealed most fully in Jesus Christ.

How do we carry out our mission in the midst of a larger culture? What is our culture, anyway? It's the television programs and commercials we and our children watch, the websites we visit, the song lyrics that flow through our ear buds, the video games we play, the movies we see, the books and blogs we read. Culture includes the kinds of work that pay handsomely and the kinds that pay poorly, how we earn our livelihood and how we spend our money, the neighborhoods we live in and the neighborhoods we avoid, the toys our children play with and who their playmates are. Culture is the quality and quantity of food we eat or can't afford to eat, the social advantages we enjoy and the social handicaps that stunt our growth, the people with whom we spend our time and the people we prefer to ignore or exclude, governmental budgets and household budgets, what and how we celebrate and what and how we mourn.

Culture, says commentator Thomas Mann, "is that incredibly varied and fluid matrix in which we live our lives. If, in this matrix, we are not at some point considered 'weird' because of our religious tradition and how we live according to that tradition, then maybe we have become too much like the Joneses."[2] Maybe we are salt that has lost its taste.

As the church, we are "called out" of our culture, not to escape, but to live in a manner consistent with the gospel. As Paul says to the church at Rome, "Don't be conformed to the patterns of this world, but be transformed by the renewing of your minds so that you can figure out what God's will is—and what is good and pleasing and mature" (Romans 12:2). As a holy people, we live *in* but not *of* the world.

That vitriolic fanaticism does not commend itself to most thoughtful believers today. We don't have to attack or disparage anyone else. But should we not affirm Deuteronomy's charge to love God with our whole selves? Should we not resist the idolatry that creeps into our own lives? Should we not be witnesses to the loving and holy character of God? Should we not honor the values that we know God honors? Should we not be a showcase of God's love and justice?

Remembering the Lord's Provision

While Moses' speech in Deuteronomy 8 is directed to the generation of Israelites who are poised to leave the wilderness and enter the Promised Land, the writer of Deuteronomy is addressing Israelites who have been in the land for centuries. For both audiences, the message has to do with God's providential care and the importance of Israel not forgetting about it.

Moses reminds his listeners that when Israel was hungry in the wilderness, the Lord provided manna for physical sustenance. But there was more to the experience than simply getting enough calories to survive. God was teaching that "people don't live on bread alone. No, they live based on whatever the LORD says" (Deuteronomy 8:3). Physical nourishment is essential, but life in its fullness requires something more.

Our lives have a spiritual dimension; our spirits need to connect with *the* Spirit. Lots of people in twenty-first-century America are seeking that connection, but not always in the right places. Deuteronomy tells us over and over again that Israel finds its true life by remembering what God has done and by keeping the commandments.

Across the Testaments

One Does Not Live by Bread Alone

Because Jesus quotes it in the temptation story (Matthew 4:1-11; Luke 4:1-13), Deuteronomy 8:3 is probably the verse of Deuteronomy most familiar to Christians. There are in fact several connections between Deuteronomy 6–8 and the accounts of Jesus' temptation. Jesus quotes not only Deuteronomy 8:3 but also 6:13 and 6:16.

Both Deuteronomy and the Gospel stories have a wilderness setting. The forty days and nights echo the forty years. Both stories have a theme of hunger and testing. Most important to the Gospel writers were the common theme of parent and child and the contrast of Israel and Jesus. Ancient Israel (the child) was frequently disobedient to God (the parent), while Jesus (the Son) keeps God's instructions. Jesus passed the test, placing his trust in God and knowing that God is the One who provides.[3]

The context for deciding whether to trust and obey is specific to each "Israel." The wilderness generation of Israel faced the decision while on the boundary between a hand-to-mouth nomadic life in the wilderness and a more secure, settled life in Canaan. The context for the decision required of the contemporaries of the writer of Deuteronomy is quite different. This "Israel" lives much later in a situation of prosperity.

These Israelites have been enjoying for some time the abundance of the land that was promised. They have grown accustomed to streams and springs, wheat and barley, vineyards and olive groves, figs and pomegranates, iron and copper (8:7-10). These Israelites (or more accurately, some of them) have plenty of food and fine houses, large herds and flocks, stashes of silver and gold (8:12-13). Is, perhaps, the test of fullness harder than the test of hunger? Will those who are comfortable remember the Giver of the good gifts they enjoy? Or will they be inclined to think, "My own strength and abilities have produced all this prosperity for me" (8:17)? So long as they have theological amnesia, they are not likely to be the faithful community that God desires.

What Does the Lord Require?

In Deuteronomy 10–11 Moses brings to a close his sermon on the great commandments before setting forth more detailed rules for living (Chapters 12–26).

Both the rhetorical question in 10:12a ("What does the LORD your God ask of you?") and the answer that follows in 10:12b-13 are reminiscent of Micah 6:6-8. The only requirement, in a nutshell, is to revere God, to walk with God, to love and serve God, and to keep the Lord's commandments. What God expects of the people is not arbitrary: "It's for your own good!" (Deuteronomy 10:13b; NRSV, "for your own well-being").

Some Christians throughout history and even today have the false impression that the religion of ancient Israel and even later Judaism is concerned only with outward behavior and not inner motivation. Deuteronomy 10:16 gives the lie to that misconception: "circumcise your hearts." Israel has always maintained that circumcised hearts—mind and will devoted to the Lord—are what God requires (see also Jeremiah 4:4; 9:26).

Circumcision of the heart is here connected to the divine concern for justice. The supreme God who is "God of all gods" and "Lord of all lords" has a special interest in the way the community treats its most vulnerable members: widows, orphans, and resident aliens (10:17-19).

Chapter 11 concludes with a challenge from Moses to Israel—and us (11:26-28). The future is full of possibilities, good and bad. What do you really want? Whom will you serve? Whom will you trust and obey?

Live the Story

Gratitude is more than a polite social convention. Social scientists have joined the ranks of pastors and theologians who recognize the effects of gratitude on mental, physical, and spiritual well-being. The ground-breaking humanistic psychologist Abraham Maslow recognized a half-century ago the capacity of gratitude to help people "appreciate again and again, freshly and naively, the basic goods of life with awe, pleasure, wonder, and even ecstasy, however stale these experiences may have become to others" as a central aspect of what he called "self-actualizing individuals."[4] Robert Emmons, a professor of psychology at the University of California, Davis, reports that recent research confirms that gratitude protects against destructive emotions such as envy, greed, resentment, bitterness, and contributes to positive emotions such as happiness, vitality, optimism, hope, and greater satisfaction with life.

The best motivation for keeping God's commandments is *thankfulness*. If we try to keep them only out of a dogged sense of duty, sooner or later our willpower grows weary. But if our motivation is gratitude for what God has done and continues to do for us, then obedience is something we *want* to do, not something we *have* to do.

What are you doing to cultivate a sense of gratitude? What might you be doing? Giving thanks to God at meals is a good start. It's not a difficult step from that to thanking God regularly for friends, for families, for homes, for jobs, for good health, and for prosperity. As your life of thanksgiving continues and deepens, do you find yourself wanting to offer prayers of gratitude, not only for the obvious blessings, but for God's sustaining presence and power? Do you want to offer prayers of gratitude when obstacles are overcome, when help is received in times of need, when comfort is offered and accepted, when opportunities for service are recognized and seized? Once in a while, do you find yourself thanking and praising God simply for being God?

1. Thomas W. Mann, *Deuteronomy*. Westminster Bible Companion (Louisville: Westminster, John Knox, 1995), 69.

2. Mann, *Deuteronomy*, 68.

3. See the discussion in Patrick D. Miller, *Deuteronomy*. Interpretation (Louisville: John Knox, 1990), 117-18.

4. Quoted by Robert A. Emmons in "The Joy of Thanks," *Spirituality and Health* magazine (Winter 2002).

4.

Open Heart and Open Hand

Deuteronomy 12:1–16:17

Claim Your Story

Becca Stevens is an Episcopal priest who serves as a university chaplain. She is also an outspoken advocate for women with criminal histories of prostitution and substance abuse. Stevens founded Nashville's Magdalene House in 1997 to provide a long-term residential community and safe haven for women who have experienced violence and addiction. Magdalene's six homes (as of 2011) provide free shelter for up to two years for twenty-eight women, most of whom were sexually abused as young girls and began using alcohol or drugs soon after. Magdalene staff members have helped more than a hundred women secure social and legal services. Observing that residents struggled to find jobs because of their criminal records, Stevens in 2001 added a bath-and-body-products enterprise, Thistle Farms. Thirty-five current and past residents earn wages and learn business skills through that nonprofit business.

Women trapped in a cycle of abuse, poverty, prostitution, and addiction are surely among the most vulnerable people in America. Becca Stevens had compassion for them and found ways to heal and restore their lives.

But there are far too many people in our society and around the world who are poor and vulnerable! Do you personally know any of them? Where does your life intersect with them? Is it when you're stopped at a traffic light and asked for a donation? Perhaps it is when you volunteer at a soup kitchen. Have you encountered the poor on a church mission trip in this country or abroad? Does the interaction happen when you are a host for homeless folks who sleep in your church during cold weather?

What connections do you see between your faith and ministry with the poor? In this session, we'll look at what the Bible has to say about poor and vulnerable people.

Enter the Bible Story

Keeping the First Commandment

The long and detailed presentation of the "regulations and the case laws" (Deuteronomy 12:1; NRSV, "statutes and ordinances"; NIV, "decrees and laws") that will run through Chapter 26 begin with a now-familiar theme: Apostasy and idolatry must be stamped out (12:1–13:18)! Deuteronomy here identifies a particular reason to justify the elimination of all traces of worship from the previous inhabitants of the land: child sacrifice (12:31).

If these laws were composed or compiled after the collapse of Jerusalem and Judah in 587 B.C., then there is a larger purpose behind these chapters. Deuteronomy is concerned about (a) how the disasters Israel had endured could have been avoided, and (b) how Israel could avoid repeating such disasters. Idolatry is seen as the chief culprit, so dangerous that it must be eradicated at any cost. As contemporary readers, we can appreciate the diagnosis of the problem without endorsing the regimen of treatment!

God's Concern for the Poor and Vulnerable

Deuteronomy 14:1-21 has to do with dietary laws, distinguishing between clean and unclean food. The rationale for these laws may seem a bit murky to today's readers. Suffice it to say that it has to do with guarding the holiness of the people of Israel in everyday life.

Much easier to understand, but perhaps more difficult to put into practice, is the concern for poor and vulnerable people reflected in Deuteronomy 14:22–15:18. When Israel as a whole is oppressed, the Lord leads them out of slavery. When Israel inherits the land, God emerges as the protector of those groups and individuals who are landless. Widows, orphans, and resident aliens are singled out for special attention.

With the loss of a primary breadwinner and with no inheritance rights, the situation of widows and orphans in ancient Israel was precarious. Immigrants (NRSV, "resident aliens"; NIV "aliens"), barred from owning land, were likewise vulnerable to economic disaster and to mistreatment. The triennial tithe was one means of providing assistance to widows, orphans, and immigrants (as well as Levites, who owned no land) on a regular basis (14:28-29).

Widows and Orphans in the New Testament

While Paul believed that Christ's return was imminent, that belief did not lead him to ignore the needs of the poor. During his travels, he took up a collection for the poor of the church in Jerusalem, which included widows (Romans 15:25-27; 1 Corinthians 16:1-4; 2 Corinthians 8:1–9:12; Galatians 2:1-10; see also Acts 6:1). To Paul's way of thinking, there should be a "fair balance" (2 Corinthians 8:14, NRSV) between those who have an abundance and those whose needs are great. Christians who have financial resources are to help those Christians who are poor.

James 1:27 provides a succinct description of authentic faith: "True devotion, the kind that is pure and faultless before God the Father, is this: to care for orphans and widows in their difficulties...." James's concern for the poor, orphans and widows in particular, hearkens back to Deuteronomy and other books of the Torah.

The triennial tithe was one of several ameliorative efforts in the Torah to respond to the needs of those living on the edge of economic disaster. In a society in which poverty and slavery were not part of God's intention and not supposed to exist, some provisions were needed to help those who had already suffered economic disaster to recover. For any number of reasons—death and disability of the breadwinner, drought, poor judgment, exploitation by those with wealth and power—peasant farmers with barely enough resources to provide for themselves and their families could slip into poverty and not be able to escape. A similar risk of ruin and destitution would have accompanied loans for commercial purposes that were common at a later stage of Israel's history. Debts accumulate and become crushing burdens. When economic hardships compounded, sometimes the only way for a poor person to survive was to become a slave.

But if God's intention is that all persons in a community should flourish, some means of breaking the cycle of poverty that keeps the poor in economic dependency is needed. The Book of Deuteronomy provides for two such radical measures.

Across the Testaments

You Always Have the Poor

Perhaps the best-known biblical passage about the poor is one frequently taken completely out of context. In three of the Gospels (Matthew 26:11; Mark 14:7; John 12:8) a verse appears on the lips of Jesus: "You always have the poor with you." That utterance is often taken as an excuse for ignoring poor people. After all, so this line of thinking goes, there is always going to be poverty; it's inevitable. But that interpretation is just the opposite of what the verse means in its Gospel context and its original context.

In the Gospel context, a woman anoints Jesus with a costly ointment. Some of those who witness her action object that the money would have been better spent alleviating the needs of the poor. Jesus replies by commending the woman's extravagant devotion. She has given silent testimony to Jesus' identity as the Messiah (which means "anointed one") and has symbolically prepared for his burial, anticipating his suffering and death for others. So in the context of these three Gospels, the point of the story is to call us to extravagant devotion to Jesus.[1]

When Jesus says, "You always have the poor with you," he is alluding to Deuteronomy 15:11: "Poor persons will never disappear from the earth." That statement, however, is preceded by an appeal for economic sharing and followed by the directive to "open your hand generously to your fellow Israelites, to the needy among you, and to the poor who live with you in your land." Far from justifying casual disregard for the poor, Jesus is presupposing that his listeners will respond to poverty within the framework of the covenant community.

Forgiveness of Debts

One of those radical measures is the stipulation that debts are to be forgiven every seven years. Deuteronomy 15:1-11 describes this feature of the Sabbatical Year.

In a land full of God's blessing and where the people obey the Lord's instruction, there should not be any people who are poor (15:4). *That* is God's intention, the way things are supposed to be. But the Bible is realistic. Inevitably, in a sinful and broken world, some people will fall into poverty (15:11). To help close the gap between the divine intention that everyone in the community should flourish economically and the recognition that some people do not, compassionate sharing is needed, expected, and even required.

Poor people are not to be considered outcasts of the society; rather they are to be regarded and accepted as neighbors. Notice how often Deuteronomy 15 refers to those in debt as a member of the community, a neighbor, or "fellow Israelites" (verses 2, 3, 7, 9, 11). The assumption is that all Israelites, whether rich or poor, belong to one family under God. One's sisters and brothers have a legitimate claim upon one's compassion and care.

Every seventh year, debts are to be cancelled so that everyone gets a fresh start, breaking the cycle of poverty. The motivation for that bold action comes from an attitude of generosity. Do not be hard-hearted (15:7) and do not entertain a mean or hostile thought toward your neighbor (15:9). Do not rationalize ignoring poor persons in the community. As biblical scholar Patrick Miller summarizes, "compassion and openheartedness are the order of God, attitudes that work themselves out in the action of the hand, which, like the heart, must be open and not closed."[2]

Release From Debt-Slavery

A second radical measure that marries conscience and legislative action to counter poverty in ancient Israel had to do with debt-slavery (15:12-14; see also Exodus 21:2; Leviticus 25:39-41). Deuteronomy calls for the release of slaves after six years, with the stipulation to provide one's newly freed slave with the material wherewithal to navigate successfully the transition to self-sufficiency. The assumption in all three passages is that, while circumstances may force people into slavery, debt-slavery is not supposed to be a permanent condition. There must be regular ways of allowing the poor to shed their burdens and chains, to recoup, to recover, to begin anew.

The purpose underlying both radical measures is to break the cycle of poverty and dependency, to restore human freedom and dignity to the poor.

Three Great Festivals

The three great pilgrimage festivals described in Deuteronomy connect the annual agricultural calendar of Israel—harvests in the spring, summer, and fall—with seasonal celebrations of major events in Israel's national history. The Festivals of Passover, Weeks, and Booths were occasions both of solemn meaning and joyous celebrations with plenty of food and fellowship.

Deuteronomy weaves together four strands of tradition into the Festival of Passover. In terms of the agricultural cycle, the Passover was originally a festival for sheep owners. The Festival of Unleavened Bread was related more directly to grain farming. In terms of religious significance, the Passover commemorated protection from the final plague unleashed against Pharaoh: the death of the firstborn (see Exodus 12:1-13). The Festival of Unleavened Bread commemorated Israel's hasty escape from Egypt, when there wasn't time to put leaven in the bread (see Exodus 13:3-10). Passover and Unleavened Bread are combined into a single, complex worship event in Deuteronomy 16:1-8.

The Festival of Weeks (Deuteronomy 16:9-12; see also Leviticus 23:15-21), which marked the grain harvest, was celebrated seven full weeks after the spring Passover (hence, it became known as *Pentecost*, from the Greek word for *fifty*). Deuteronomy 16:12 explicitly connects this celebration with the remembrance of the Israelites in Egypt. Tradition after the Babylonian Exile associated this feast with the giving of the Ten Commandments at Mount Sinai/Horeb. That association was probably based on Exodus 19:1, which reports that the Israelites entered the wilderness of Sinai in the third month after leaving Egypt. Weeks or Pentecost was celebrated in the third month of the Jewish religious calendar.

Two details warrant brief comment. First, the amount of the offering made by each Israelite head of household was to be chosen voluntarily; it was a "spontaneous gift" (16:10), prompted by gratitude for the blessing received from God.

Passover and Pentecost in the New Testament

The Passover appears several places in the New Testament. Luke 2:41-42 reports that when he was twelve years old, Jesus came to Jerusalem with his parents for the Passover Festival. The Gospel of John reports that it was the time of Passover when Jesus cleared the Jerusalem Temple of people engaged in commerce (John 2:13-25). The Synoptic Gospels present Jesus' Last Supper with his disciples as a Passover meal (Matthew 26:17-30; Mark 14:12-25; Luke 22:7-23). According to the Gospel of John, Jesus' final meal with his disciples, when he washed their feet, was "before the Festival of Passover" (John 13:1-2a). John 19:14 reports that Pilate brought Jesus before the Jewish leaders for judgment "about noon on the Preparation Day for the Passover." That timing suggests that Jesus, whom the Fourth Evangelist calls the "Lamb of God" (John 1:29), was crucified as the Passover lambs were being slaughtered.

Acts 2:1-4 reports that Jesus' followers had gathered at the time of Pentecost, when they were filled with the Holy Spirit. Therefore, Pentecost continues to have special significance in the Christian church.

Second, *everyone* was invited to this party! The celebratory meal included every member of a family, men and women, sons and daughters. Slaves were also participants, along with Levites and the most impoverished folks in the community: immigrants, orphans, and widows (16:11). Christian readers cannot help but recall Jesus' counsel that when we host a banquet we should invite "the poor, crippled, lame, and blind"—the people in the community who can't return the social favor (Luke 14:12-14).

The Festival of Booths (Deuteronomy 16:13-15; also know as *Sukkoth* or *Tabernacles*) coincided with the grape and olive harvests in early autumn. Celebrated for seven days, its most distinctive feature is the requirement to sleep in rough, temporary shelters in remembrance of the wandering in the wilderness after leaving Egypt (see Leviticus 23:39-43). The Festival of Booths was an opportunity for fellowship and rejoicing. Everyone in a household, including slaves, was expected to participate, along with the landless members of the community: Levites, widows, orphans, and immigrants.

Live the Story

So where do you go from here? What are you going to do? What kind of person are you going to be? What are the next steps? What might be the next steps for you? For your congregation? Here are some possibilities:

Personal Education. While information by itself is not sufficient for faithful living, information *is* necessary. The counsel of the great Jewish thinker Martin Buber is instructive in this regard: "The graver the crisis becomes the more earnest and consciously responsible is the knowledge demanded of us; for although what is demanded is a deed, only that deed which is born of knowledge will help to overcome the crisis."[3] Pay attention to news stories about the poor and needy. Find out what information is available through your church. Seek out websites that address issues that affect poor and marginalized people.

Leadership. Look for ways that you can raise awareness in your congregation of poverty issues. Perhaps you could be a member of the social outreach or mission program committee in your congregation. Might you organize or join a committee to address poverty issues through your church's regional network?

Direct Services. This involves direct action to meet the immediate needs of poor people. Volunteer at a food bank, a clothes bank, a soup kitchen, a shelter for homeless persons, a Habitat for Humanity build, a school in an underprivileged neighborhood that needs tutors, or visit inmates in a jail or prison.

Simpler Living. Are you ready to make lifestyle changes to reduce your level of consumption? If those changes save you money, devote that savings to ministry with the poor. If you make changes that mean you can work for pay fewer hours, devote some of those hours saved to ministry with the poor.

Financial Contributions. Support efforts through your congregation and your denomination to alleviate poverty or to respond to a particular need. Support other organizations that do that work on a local, national, or international level.

Global Solidarity. Get involved in projects that alleviate poverty while building relationships with poor people in other countries.

Legislative Advocacy. Get involved with a group or network working to influence poverty-related public policy at the local, state, or national level.

You will learn only from experience which step is right for you now . . . and which will be the right *next* step. Wherever you begin, whatever you do next, remember that "Christ has no body but yours."

Christ Has No Body

Christ has no body but yours,
No hands, no feet on earth but yours,
Yours are the eyes with which he looks
Compassion on this world,
Yours are the feet with which he walks to do good,
Yours are the hands, with which he blesses all the world.
Yours are the hands, yours are the feet,
Yours are the eyes, you are his body.
Christ has no body now but yours,
No hands, no feet on earth but yours,
Yours are the eyes with which he looks
compassion on this world.
Christ has no body now on earth but yours.
    —Commonly attributed to Teresa of Avila (1515–1582)

1. See Richard B. Hays, "You Always Have the Poor with You," *Biblical Literacy Today*, 3:2 (Winter 1988-89), 3.

2. Patrick D. Miller, *Deuteronomy*. Interpretation (Louisville: John Knox, 1990), 136.

3. Martin Buber, *Paths in Utopia*. Translated by R.F. C. Hull (New York: Macmillan, 1950), 129.

5.

Grand Central Story

Deuteronomy 6:20-25; 16:18–26:15

Claim Your Story

The ancient Greek maxim "Know Thyself," inscribed at the temple of Apollo at Delphi and famously employed by Socrates, has a timeless quality. The dictum is deceptively simple. But how do you give more than a simplistic answer? How *do* you go about knowing yourself?

One way we know who we are is to tell our *story*. The personal stories of ordinary Americans recorded as part of the StoryCorps project (and available on National Public Radio) help to tell who those Americans are. The StoryCorps project includes the story of the daughter of the Italian immigrant who was the chief stone carver at Mount Rushmore, the story of the man who was the first black student at Louisiana State University (going on to a long and successful career in special education and receiving an honorary doctorate from LSU), the story of the middle-school science teacher who inspired his student to become a neurosurgeon, and others.

We also know who we are by telling the larger stories to which we belong. For instance, as Americans, we claim the Declaration of Independence as *our* story. That document reflects not merely the convictions of a group of aristocratic men gathered in Philadelphia in the summer of 1776; it expresses our convictions, too. *We* "hold these truths to be self-evident, that all men are created equal, that they are endowed by their Creator with certain unalienable Rights, that among these are Life, Liberty and the pursuit of Happiness."

Our journey as Americans has required some midcourse corrections. We claim these as part of our story, too, part of who we are. In his address at Gettysburg, Abraham Lincoln wasn't speaking only to his contemporaries gathered at the scene of a horribly bloody battle; he was speaking to and for *us*. Lincoln told the story of who *we* are as a nation. "Fourscore and seven years ago our fathers brought forth on this continent a new nation, conceived in Liberty, and dedicated to the proposition that all men are created equal." Our story was unfinished at that point, of course. There was "unfinished work" to be done, a "great task remaining before us." We as a nation are still working to complete that task and to realize our identity.

The Women's Suffrage Movement, led by Mary Cady Stanton, Susan B. Anthony, Lucretia Mott, and Lucy Stone, among others, represents another midcourse correction to our story. It took decades of protest, demonstrations, conventions, editorials, debates, and lobbying to ensure that women would win the right to vote. In 1920, that goal became the law of the land with ratification of the Nineteenth Amendment, prohibiting gender-based restrictions on voting. The struggle for full economic equality for women remains a national aspiration yet to be achieved.

The work and the story reached another high-water mark when Martin Luther King, Jr. stood on the steps of the Lincoln Memorial to deliver his famous "I Have a Dream" speech. King was explicitly calling for another midcourse correction to our national story. "Five score years ago, a great American, in whose symbolic shadow we stand, signed the Emancipation Proclamation. . . . It came as a joyous daybreak to the long night of captivity. But one hundred years later, we must face the tragic fact that the Negro is still not free." King went on to say that "*now* is the time" to embody true democracy, racial justice, and opportunity for "all of God's children." King's dream has been embraced by the American people as *our* shared dream. A half-century after the March on Washington, we are still trying to make reality match the dream. But in our finer moments, Americans recognize that King articulated our story; it tells us who we are and the kind of people we want to be.

The Book of Deuteronomy is telling the story of the people of Israel. More than that, Deuteronomy is encouraging the people of God to keep retelling the story and to embody it in their common life. It is as if Deuteronomy is saying, "This is who you are! You have a relationship with God. Why haven't you acted like it? Start acting like it!"

Enter the Bible Story

Grand Central Story

Biblical scholar and pastor Thomas Mann has suggested that each of us has a "grand central story," a central story that serves as the organizing center for all the other stories in our lives. Such a grand central story shapes our beliefs, our values, and the way we live.

Powerful stories do more than entertain us; they transform us, they reshape our identity and our perceptions of the world and what is important. That's true of our personal stories and of our cultural stories. The story that most captivates our imagination profoundly shapes who we are and what we will do and will not do.

Deuteronomy 26:5-10 is Israel's grand central story. This retelling of the story comes near the end of the formal law code in the context of instructions for the offering of first fruits of the harvest. These verses are a kind of confession of faith, a concise creed jam-packed with meaning. I want to call attention to five points.

First, the "starving Aramean" (26:5; NRSV, "wandering Aramean") refers to Jacob, who fled the famine in Canaan and moved to Egypt. The number of his descendants exploded, but they remained "immigrants" (NRSV, "aliens"), powerless and vulnerable to abuse. Note the change in pronouns from verse 5 to verse 6 and following; "he" becomes "we" and "us." The retelling of the story reinforces a bridge and a bond between generations. We love to tell the old, old story because it is our story, too.

Second, Pharaoh enslaved the Hebrews (26:6), and when they cried for help, the Lord heard their voices, saw their misery, and intervened (26:7-8). God did not tolerate oppression without end, but worked actively for the liberation of the downtrodden (with "awesome power" and "signs and wonders").

Third, God provided the Israelites with a fertile land so they could support themselves and not fall back into slavery (26:9). The gift of the land was essential to breaking the cycle of oppression and poverty.

Fourth, throughout the time while the Book of Deuteronomy was being composed and compiled, the threat of losing the land was very real. In the eighth century B.C., the Assyrians ravaged the Northern Kingdom of Israel. By the sixth century B.C., Babylon had done its worst and Jerusalem controlled very little of the territory that had been claimed by David and Solomon. By remembering the gracious purpose and power that had created Israel in the first place, Deuteronomy offered a basis of hope for the future.

Finally, the recital of the mighty acts of God in Israel's early history is woven into the instruction about a harvest thank offering for the bounty of the land (26:10). This grand central story recognizes the Lord God as ruler of both *history* and *nature*.

Another Summary

Israel's grand central story is summarized also in Deuteronomy 6:20-25, where its intergenerational character and its connection to the instruction of the Lord by means of the law are emphasized. "In the future, your children will ask you, 'What is the meaning of the laws, the regulations, and the case laws that the LORD our God commanded you?'" The answer is to tell again the story of God bringing the people out of Egypt and into the land of Canaan.

There is no conflict in Israel's grand central story between law and grace. It is because the Lord—who has already brought the Israelites out of Egypt and into the Promised Land—is gracious that God gives the law. It is not meant as a burden on the people but "that things go well for us always" (6:24; NRSV, "for our lasting good; NIV, "always prosper and be kept alive"). Just as we Americans recognize that living in a society under the rule of law is a life of freedom and privilege, so it is with the ancient Israelites whom Deuteronomy addressed.

The law (which is God's instruction) becomes part of Israel's grand central story. The law helps to create and sustain a people of a particular character—both as individuals and as a community. Think for a moment how a parent trying to shape a young child's behavior and character sometimes says, "That's something that we simply don't do in our family" or "Doing this [particular positive activity] is part of our family tradition. It's who we are." The law given to Israel functions in a similar way. It provides instruction that says, in effect: *"This* is the kind of people we are." *"This* is the kind of community we are." *"This* is the way we behave." "We don't do *that* sort of thing." "We encourage *this* kind of behavior, *that* way of relating to each other and to God." *"This* is important in our community." "We've discovered that doing *this* and avoiding *that* helps us flourish."

Justice, Justice, and Only Justice

Justice is something essential, Deuteronomy says, if persons and communities are to flourish. Moses' direction about judges and officials in Deuteronomy 16:18-20 echoes his earlier instruction in Deuteronomy 1:12-17. The maintenance of justice is a core value of the covenant community, the importance of which cannot be overstated. "Justice, and only justice, you shall pursue" (16:20, NRSV; NIV, "follow justice and justice alone"). For Deuteronomy, the denial of justice was an offense to God comparable to worshiping other gods. The prophetic books of the Bible attest that the subversion of justice was not a merely "academic" matter (see, for example, Isaiah 10:1-2; Amos 5:15; Micah 2:1-2).

Doing justice has ramifications for the way a community or a society treats its weakest members. Running through the Book of Deuteronomy, and in fact through the entire Torah, is the motif that helping the most disadvantaged members of society is a primary religious obligation. The legal traditions in the Torah stipulate certain rights of the poor and corresponding duties of more successful members of the community. For instance, employers are prohibited from withholding the wages of day laborers (24:14-15; see also Leviticus 19:13). The legal provision for gleaning required that landowners not be excessively efficient in harvesting

Across the Testaments

Eye for Eye, Tooth for Tooth

The *lex talionus*, Latin for the "law of retribution," appears in slightly different forms in three places in the Old Testament: Exodus 21:23-25; Leviticus 24:18-20; Deuteronomy 19:21. In the first two instances, the intent is to curb unlimited private revenge (see, for example, Genesis 4:23-24) by building into Israel's law code the requirement that punishment must be proportionate to the harm inflicted. The guilty should suffer retribution that is equivalent to the injury caused. The punishment should fit, not exceed, the crime.

The context of the law of retribution in Deuteronomy 19:15-21 is different. The focus is not on how to deal with violent acts but on how to deal with perjury. Witnesses whose testimony is untruthful and malicious undermine the entire system of legal justice, so harsh, dissuasive measures were seen as necessary.

In the Sermon on the Mount Jesus tells his listeners, "'You have heard that it was said, *An eye for an eye and a tooth for a tooth*. But I say to you that you must not oppose those who want to hurt you'" (Matthew 5:38-39, my emphasis added in this paragraph; some scholars translate verse 39 as "Do not use violence to resist an evil-doer"). A few verses later in the Sermon, Jesus says, "You have heard that it was said, *You must love your neighbor* and hate your enemy. But I say to you, love your enemies ..." (5:43-44). Jesus is telling his followers (then and now) how to live in the present-and-coming divine Kingdom. In that Kingdom, enemies are not seen as merely enemies, but as neighbors to be loved. In the new Kingdom that Jesus announces, his disciples will embrace even enemies, imitating God's love and mercy for all.

crops (24:19-22; see also Leviticus 19:9-10; 23:22). Gleaning provided a double benefit for poor members of the community. Along with the food gathered, gleaning—because it required work—provided the poor with a degree of dignity. The third-year tithe was one means of providing assistance to poor people (as well as to Levites, who owned no land) on a regular basis (14:28-29; 26:12-15). Perhaps even more significant was the practice of extending interest-free loans (23:19-20; see also Exodus 22:25; Leviticus 25:35-38). When a loan to a poor person involves collateral, the Torah is explicit in protecting both the physical well-being and the dignity of the one borrowing (24:10-13; see also Exodus 22:26-27).

How Should a King Behave?

Every grand central story of a people entails some sort of polity, some way of organizing society, some way of making decisions, some pattern of leaders and followers. Israel began as a tribal confederacy and later became a monarchy. Moses' speech in Deuteronomy 17:14-20 is presented as instruction to the people who are about to enter the Promised Land about how a future king of Israel should and should not behave.

The Book of Deuteronomy is written from the later vantage point of someone who has witnessed the good and the bad in Israel's royal leadership. Moses says that the king "must not acquire too many horses" (17:16), but the Deuteronomy writer knows that Solomon "had forty thousand horse stalls for his chariots and twelve thousand additional horses" (1 Kings 4:26). Moses warns that "the king must not take numerous wives so that his heart [his religious loyalty] doesn't go astray" (17:17a). In sharp contrast to the ideal, Solomon's entanglements with the pagan religions of his "seven hundred royal wives and three hundred secondary wives" did just what Moses feared. Those marriages, which cemented political alliances, compromised Solomon's exclusive devotion to the Lord; "his wives turned his heart after other gods" (1 Kings 11:3-4). Moses cautions that having a king who acquires large quantities of gold and silver is bound to lead to problems. The writer of Deuteronomy knows that Solomon had accumulated a fortune of legendary proportions (see 1 Kings 10:14-22).

In short, Moses presciently admonishes the people of Israel to be wary of any king with unchecked military power, a pattern of political and religious compromises, and massive wealth.

If those are the royal vices to be avoided, what are the positive virtues of the ideal king? Deuteronomy emphasizes above all that he is to be a zealous student and observer of God's commandments. Deferring to God's ultimate sovereignty and not counting himself above the law, the ideal king will have certain humility. He will not see himself as superior in status and privilege to his fellow citizens (Deuteronomy 17:18-20).

The American political context in the twenty-first century is obviously very different from the theocratic context of ancient Israel. But is there still some relevance for us today in Deuteronomy's criteria for assessing leadership? Shouldn't we be asking ourselves, does vast wealth or controlling power contribute to good leadership or contaminate it? What are the dangers when a leader believes he or she is above the law? Do we want an imperial leader or a covenantal leader? How might a leader give evidence of a healthy measure of humility? Nations and empires, some with monarchs and some with presidents, rise and fall. But what qualities of leadership seem to transcend time and place? What sort of leaders do we want?

Levirate Marriage Law

Israel's grand central story encompassed social rules of a very practical nature. Deuteronomy 25:5-10 describes an arrangement often called *levirate* marriage (from the Latin *levir* = brother-in-law). If a man died without a male heir, the law urged (but did not absolutely require) the brother of the deceased man to marry the widow and produce a son who would be counted as the original husband's firstborn for purposes of inheritance. In this decidedly patriarchal society, this law provided a way to perpetuate male lineage. But it simultaneously served to protect widows, who would otherwise be left in a vulnerable position.

Across the Testaments

Jesus and Levirate Marriage

This statute from Deuteronomy provides the basis for the Sadducees' effort to entrap Jesus (Matthew 22:23-33; Mark 12:18-27; Luke 20:27-40) with an imagined scenario: If a woman has been widowed several times and has consequently married seven brothers, whose wife will she be in the resurrection? The Sadducees (unlike the Pharisees) denied the reality of a general resurrection and therefore presented a situation designed to make the idea look ridiculous while boxing Jesus into a corner.

Jesus sidesteps any comment about the appropriateness of levirate marriage law in everyday life. He demolishes the Sadducees' trap by insisting that God's power extends even over death. The resurrection-life, Jesus says, is not a mere reflection of life in this mundane age. Gender roles will be overcome; the primary identity of women, no less than men, will not be in terms of spousal relationships.

Live the Story

Christians have a grand central story, too. Our story is rooted in the Old Testament because we have been grafted onto the story of redemption extending from Abraham and Sarah through the prophets (see Romans 11:17-24). Our story continues in the New Testament in the story of Jesus, whom the early church came to recognize as Messiah and Lord (see, for example, Acts 10:36; Romans 8:38-39; 10:9; 1 Corinthians 1:9; 8:6; 2 Corinthians 4:5; Philippians 2:11).

The story is not just an old story, but a *living* story. We continue to tell the story of Jesus when we sing a favorite hymn:

I love to tell the story of unseen things above,
of Jesus and his glory, of Jesus and his love.
I love to tell the story, because I know 'tis true;
it satisfies my longings as nothing else can do.[1]

We continue to tell our story whenever we recite the Apostles' Creed, which sets the story of who Jesus is and what he has done within a framework of conviction about the triune God, the life of the church, and the life everlasting. We reclaim the story of Jesus each time we hear the gospel read and preached, each time we participate in a baptism or in the Lord's Supper. We live the story of Jesus whenever we reach out with compassion and generosity to "the least of these" whom Christ loves (see Matthew 25:31-46).

What is *your congregation* doing to claim and embody the Christian story? What are *you* doing to claim the story as your own? How is the Christian story shaping *you*? What are *you* doing to help your children and their generation join the story? What more are you ready to do?

---

1. Words by Katherine Hankey, *The United Methodist Hymnal* (Nashville: The United Methodist Publishing House, 1989), 156.

6.

Choose Life!

Deuteronomy 26:16–34:12

Claim Your Story

Ponder for a few minutes the most important personal commitments you have made. Perhaps those include a special friendship with someone, a deep and lasting bond of fellowship and caring. Maybe what comes to mind immediately is your commitment to a life partner, in which you pledged fidelity throughout an unknown future. Perhaps you have adopted a child, choosing to do everything in your power to protect and nurture a young life. You may have a strong sense of being called to a vocation that you are determined to live out. Maybe you are a naturalized citizen who has taken an oath of allegiance to the United States, making explicit a promise of loyalty to our nation.

What does it take to honor your commitments over time? How do you keep the most important promises you make? Why does our fervor to remain faithful to important commitments sometimes cool? What can you do to keep your most important personal commitments? What can you do to keep from breaking your most important promises?

The Book of Deuteronomy is very much concerned with making right decisions at pivotal points in our individual and collective lives and making right decisions on a recurring basis. Thus Deuteronomy speaks to us about the most important choices we make.

Enter the Bible Story

A Covenant Across Time and Geography

Deuteronomy has a powerful sense of the continuity of Israel over time and across geography. The promises God makes to one generation are promises made to every generation. The demands God makes of one generation are demands made of every generation. The covenantal relationship God establishes with one generation is a relationship offered to every generation.

Evidence of that sense of continuity is sprinkled liberally throughout the Book of Deuteronomy in the frequent use of the expression "this day" or "today" (NRSV) and "this very moment" or "right now" (CEB) in the context of the covenant with the Lord or the commandments of the Lord. Deuteronomy presents past events as contemporaneous with later readers. The opportunity for a covenantal relationship with God—and the responsibility that that entails—is available to every generation. In a sense, each generation must choose to accept the invitation.

Look, for instance, at Deuteronomy 26:16–27:10, which includes Moses' conclusion to the law code and the erecting of a memorial to the law at the time Israel crossed the Jordan River. "*This very day* the LORD is commanding you to observe these statutes and ordinances" (26:16, NRSV; my emphasis in this paragraph and the next). "*Today* you have affirmed that the LORD will be your God . . ." (26:17). "*Today* the LORD has gotten your agreement that you will be his treasured people..." (26:18). "Keep all of the commandment that I am giving you *right now*" (27:1). "Set up these stones that I'm telling you about *right now*" (27:4). "*This very moment* you have become the people of the LORD your God" (27:9). "So obey the LORD your God's voice. Do his commandments and his regulations that I'm giving you *right now*" (27:10).

As another example, consider Deuteronomy 29:2-28, which reports the covenant renewal on the plains of Moab. "*Right now*, all of you are in the presence of the LORD your God . . ." (29:10). The purpose of the gathering is "enter into the LORD your God's covenant and into the agreement that the LORD your God is making with you *right now*. That means the

Lord will make you his own people *right now* . . ." (29:12-13). The point is made unmistakably clear that all generations of Israel—past, present, and future—are included in the covenant. "I'm not making this covenant and this agreement with you alone but also with those standing here with us *right now* before the LORD our God, and also with those who aren't here with us *right now*" (29:14-15).

The inclusiveness of the covenant community extends not only across generations, embracing the people of Israel wherever they may be living at the moment, but across social distinctions. The people of God includes tribal leaders, elders, officials, men, women, children, immigrants, "the ones who chop your wood and those who draw your water." Everyone in the community, male and female, senior and junior, exalted and menial, enters into the covenant with God (29:10-13).

Acts of God?

Deuteronomy 28, with its list of blessings that will follow obedience and longer list of curses that will follow disobedience, gives us a clear sense of Deuteronomy's notion of the moral calculus that governs the universe. Toe the line and follow the divine rules for living and things will go well for you and your descendants. Veer off the straight and narrow and you and your extended family will suffer calamity.

Up to a point, we can appreciate the logic of the arrangement. We may especially like the part about natural bounty being directly linked to divine blessing—at least we like it if we are the recipients of that bounty. Some of us may wonder why the wicked and the selfish seem to do so well for themselves. But we recognize that actions normally have consequences. And everyday experience confirms that children and grandchildren *do* suffer as a result of irresponsible parenting.

But wait a minute! Deuteronomy goes further than that, believing that history is the stage and God is the heavenly director. Nations and armies are instruments of God's judgment and fearsome punishment. Deuteronomy goes even further: The forces of nature are at God's disposal and are used to reward and punish. Drought, by this reckoning, expresses

About the Christian Faith

Justification and Sanctification

After all the warnings of punishment to come to the generation entering the Promised Land if they disobey God, and all the reminders of punishment already experienced by the later audience of Deuteronomy (see 27:11-26; 28:15-68; 29:22-28), Deuteronomy 30:1-10 conveys a message of hope for the future. Disobedience inevitably leads to punishment, but *curse* is not the final word. Blessing and obedience are still possible.

Deuteronomy knows all too well that the people are prone to disobedience; they can't save themselves. But God initiates the internal change that makes obedience *possible*. Blessing and obedience are possible because the Lord "will circumcise your hearts and the hearts of your descendants so that you love the LORD your God with all your mind and with all your being" (30:6). God makes it possible for us to change our ways of acting by changing our hearts and minds.

Christians use the language of *justification* to describe this. We are restored to a right relationship with God not by our own efforts but by what God does for us. We are reconciled to God not because we have earned it but because of what God has already done for us in Jesus Christ.

But it doesn't stop there. Grace leads to gratitude and gratitude to faithful response. If our faith is genuine, we *will* change. As Deuteronomy says, "You will change and obey the LORD's voice and do all his commandments" (30:8). Christians talk about this process as *sanctification*. Restored to a healthy relationship with God, the Holy Spirit continues to work in us, enabling us to grow in holiness of heart and life.

divine judgment of human wrongdoing. Insect infestations, floods, earthquakes, and more are expressions of a divine displeasure. Worst of all, if Deuteronomy is right, epidemics that cripple entire populations are the just deserts of people doing something profoundly wrong.

Do you buy into that worldview? Or does it trouble you? Doesn't it strike you as cruel to tell people who are suffering that there is a direct connection between natural disasters and their behavior? Surely the Book of Job effectively demolishes such easy assumptions about suffering and guilt!

We can appreciate Deuteronomy's desire to explain the calamities that befell Israel (especially the loss of the land and political independence) and to warn against future calamities. We recognize that nothing good came of Israel's collective drift into idolatry and oppression of the poor. Individuals clearly suffered because of that moral drift, but thoughtful contemporary readers recognize that individual suffering is not always the result of individual sin. Real life is messier than that.

Is there anything else salvageable in Deuteronomy's system of sanctions, of blessings and curses? Maybe one of Deuteronomy's insights is that an entire society can be wrong, and when it is, the consequences can be devastating for generations. Racism and environmental degradation are two obvious examples in our own society. Perceiving and acknowledging that a society is morally and spiritually off course is not easy; it is the work of prophets, not fore-tellers so much as forth-tellers, who can read the signs of the times against the standards of God.

Is God's Law Impossible to Know and Follow?

Deuteronomy insists the law is not something so abstract or ethereal or complicated that it is too difficult for ordinary people to understand. Nor is the law so demanding that it is impossible to follow. Quite the opposite! God's word in the commandments and statutes in this book "is definitely not too difficult for you. It isn't unreachable" (30:11). It's not far

---

Across the Testaments

Blessing and Obedience and the Prodigal Son

Deuteronomy 30 raises a theological version of the perennial which-comes-first-the-chicken-or-the-egg question. Will Israel's fortune improve because it is God's nature to forgive? Or does Israel have to change first by repenting? Deuteronomy seems to say that grace and response are simultaneous; each needs the other for completion. God wants to accept the people, but that can't happen until the people act like they want to be accepted.

Deuteronomy's message resonates with Jesus' parable of the prodigal son (Luke 15:11-32). The loving father never gives up hoping and waiting to welcome his son back. But reconciliation cannot happen until the son chooses to return to the father.

away. "Not at all! The word is very close to you. It's in your mouth and your heart, waiting for you to do it" (30:14). Any person—in any generation—who diligently studies the teaching of Moses can learn it and make it a part of his or her life.

Choose Life!

The Book of Deuteronomy reaches a climax in Chapter 30, verses 15-20, which underscores that entering the covenant with the Lord requires a decision. Again, we see the frequent use of "today"/ "right now" (verses 15, 16, 18, 19), a clue that the call to decision is issued to every generation. The need to make a decision is inescapable, and the consequences momentous.

Deuteronomy is telling the reader in so many words that the *means* have to be consistent with the *ends*. It is not possible to choose life and human flourishing as the desired outcome without simultaneously choosing the way of life that leads to that result. If the people of God obey God's voice and live according to the Lord's instruction, then they will not merely survive but will flourish. But if the people decide that they can find a better life by following some other god or gods and by living according to some other set of rules and values than those provided by the Lord God, then the people will pay a terrible price. Instead of life and prosperity, they will have chosen death and adversity.

Which loyalty and lifestyle will the people choose? When Joshua issues a challenge to the people to choose a life of faithfulness to God, the response is positive (Joshua 24:14-24). But Deuteronomy doesn't tell the reader what response Moses' challenge elicited. The future is left open, waiting for readers—then and now—to decide.

A New Leader

What happens when a charismatic leader leaves a church or some other organization? How do the people who have lost their leader feel? What is the prevailing mood when someone upon whom people have depended for vision, direction, and motivation is gone? Even under the best of circumstances, replacing a key leader can be difficult. In times of crisis, it can be traumatic.

Deuteronomy narrates the passing of the mantle of leadership from Moses to Joshua (31:1-8, 14-15, 23). The community needs a new leader, obviously, someone who can be an instrument of God's leadership. But overcoming the people's fear and anxiety requires more than a human figure. One thing above all others, says Deuteronomy, is needed for a successful transition. Through Moses' voice (and the written words of Deuteronomy) members of the community of faith are reassured that God will not abandon them. The words of encouragement spoken to Joshua provide encouragement to the entire community. "The LORD is the one who is marching before you! He is the one who will be with you! He won't let you down. He won't abandon you. So don't be afraid or scared!" (31:8). Confidence that God will be present in the future just as in the past makes it possible for Israel to face the future. When the time finally comes that Moses, after a glimpse from afar of the Promised Land, dies and is buried in Moab (34:1-8), Joshua takes over as his successor (34:9; see also Joshua 1:1-9).

Across the Testaments

Leave Vengeance to God

After God has used Israel's enemies to punish Israel's rebellious behavior (32:18-21), the tide changes. The Lord now promises to exact "revenge" (32:35; NRSV, "vengeance") against those enemies.

In his letter to the church at Rome, the apostle Paul cites Deuteronomy 32:35 in his admonition to his readers, "Don't try to get revenge for yourselves, my dear friends," but leave it to God. "It is written, *Revenge belongs to me; I will pay it back, says the Lord*" (Romans 12:19; see also Hebrews 10:30). Paul is not threatening the offending party so much as warning Christians to leave judgment to God. Roman culture in Paul's time admired the wronged person who retaliated—not so different from those in our society who proclaim, "I don't get mad; I get even." Paul's counsel couldn't be more different: "If your enemy is hungry, feed him; if he is thirsty, give him a drink. By doing this, you will pile burning coals of fire upon his head. Don't be defeated by evil, but defeat evil with good" (Romans 12:20-21).

Confidence that God is trustworthy in all circumstances makes it possible for us, too, to face the twenty-first century with courage. We, too, proclaim, "God is with us. We are not alone. Thanks be to God."[1]

The Song of Moses

While Chapter 33 is Moses' own final words of blessing to the people, Deuteronomy 31:30–32:47 is explicitly identified as the final message that the Lord has instructed Moses to give as a "poem" (CEB) or "song" (NRSV, NIV) to the people (see 31:19). After Moses reminds the people of (1) God's gracious care (32:7-14), (2) their rebellious response (32:15-18), (3) the Lord's judgment (32:19-27), and (4) their acquittal to come (32:34-43), Moses urges the people to "Set your mind on all these words I'm testifying against you *right now*" (32:46, my emphasis). Teach them to coming generations so that they, too, can choose life.

One of the most striking features of Moses' poem/song is its variety of images for God. God is a *rock* (32:4, 15, 18, 30-31) for Israel, a place of refuge in an uncertain world. The Lord is a *warrior* with a "blazing sword" (32:41) and whose "arrows drink much blood" (32:42). *Parent-child* imagery is found in 32:5-6, 19-20. The Lord's providential care is like that of an *eagle* (32:11), which protects and nurtures its young. The juxtaposition of *maternal* and *paternal* images is especially powerful. God is like a rock that has sired Israel (32:18a) and like a mother who has given birth to God's people (32:18b).

Live the Story

Deuteronomy urges its readers, the Israelites and us, to love God and to do the things that keep us loving God. How might that connect with your life? Since we are to love the Lord with our whole self, every aspect of your life that came to mind as you read the opening section of this session is relevant here. It is perfectly legitimate (and helpful) to ask yourself, "What am I doing—as a friend, in my family, in my vocation, as a citizen—to choose life?"

As participants in a community of believers, Christians choose life through baptism and through confirmation of that baptism. When a parent or sponsor brings an infant or small child to be baptized, the adult promises to live a godly life and to nurture the child in Christian faith and life. When an older child or an adult is baptized, that person promises to keep God's commandments and to live as a faithful member of the church. In those church traditions that celebrate confirmation of full church membership, the candidates pledge to support the church by their prayers, their presence, their gifts, their service, and their witness. On all three of these occasions, the congregation as a whole makes a commitment to support the new brother or sister in Christ in every way possible.

We Christians make these solemn promises at pivotal times in our lives. We are baptized only once. We are confirmed as a full member of a church at a particular point in our lives. But we renew and reclaim those promises again and again across the days and months and years. We choose life once and for all—and we keep choosing life over and over in word and deed.

Renowned preacher Fred Craddock uses a monetary analogy to describe what faithfulness means in practical terms: "To give my life for Christ appears glorious," he says. "To pour myself out for others . . . to pay the ultimate price of martyrdom—I'll do it. I'm ready, Lord, to go out in a blaze of glory.... We think giving our all to the Lord is like taking a $1,000 bill and laying it on the table—'Here's my life, Lord. I'm giving it all.' But the reality for most of us is that he sends us to the bank and has us cash in the $1,000 for quarters. We go through life putting out 25 cents here and 50 cents there. Listen to the neighbor kid's troubles instead of saying, 'Get lost.' Go to a committee meeting. Give a cup of water to a shaky old man in a nursing home. Usually giving our life to Christ isn't glorious. It's done in all those little acts of love, 25 cents at a time. It would be easy to go out in a flash of glory; it's harder to live the Christian life little by little over the long haul."[2]

If you really want to choose a life of faithfulness, then you will want to make the *everyday choices* that help you keep that commitment. If you truly want to choose a way of living that is congruent with God's purposes, then you will want to do the *little things* that are compatible with that goal. What are those little things? What are those daily choices? What will you do to spend your quarters wisely? What will you do to choose life . . . each and every day?

1. See "A Statement of Faith of the United Church of Canada," *The United Methodist Hymnal* (Nashville: The United Methodist Publishing House, 1989), 883.

2. Quoted by Darryl Bell, "Practical Implications of Consecration," *Bible.org*, http://bible.org/illustration/practical-implications-consecration.

Leader Guide

People often view the Bible as a maze of obscure people, places, and events from centuries ago and struggle to relate it to their daily lives. IMMERSION invites us to experience the Bible as a record of God's loving revelation to humankind. These studies recognize our emotional, spiritual, and intellectual needs and welcome us into the Bible story and into deeper faith.

As leader of an IMMERSION group, you will help participants to encounter the Word of God and the God of the Word that will lead to new creation in Christ. You do not have to be an expert to lead; in fact, you will participate with your group in listening to and applying God's life-transforming Word to your lives. You and your group will explore the building blocks of the Christian faith through key stories, people, ideas, and teachings in every book of the Bible. You will also explore the bridges and points of connection between the Old and New Testaments.

Choosing and Using the Bible

The central goal of IMMERSION is engaging the members of your group with the Bible in a way that informs their minds, forms their hearts, and transforms the way they live out their Christian faith. Participants will need this study book and a Bible. IMMERSION is an excellent accompaniment to the Common English Bible (CEB). It shares with the CEB four common aims: clarity of language, faith in the Bible's power to transform lives, the emotional expectation that people will find the love of God, and the rational expectation that people will find the knowledge of God.

Other recommended study Bibles include *The New Interpreter's Study Bible* (NRSV), *The New Oxford Annotated Study Bible* (NRSV), *The HarperCollins Study Bible* (NRSV), the *NIV and TNIV Study Bibles*, and the *Archaeological Study Bible* (NIV). Encourage participants to use more than one translation. *The Message: The Bible in Contemporary Language* is a modern paraphrase of the Bible, based on the original languages. Eugene H. Peterson has created a masterful presentation of the Scripture text, which is best used alongside rather than in place of the CEB or another primary English translation.

One of the most reliable interpreters of the Bible's meaning is the Bible itself. Invite participants first of all to allow Scripture to have its say. Pay attention to context. Ask questions of the text. Read every passage with curiosity, always seeking to answer the basic Who? What? Where? When? and Why? questions.

Bible study groups should also have handy essential reference resources in case someone wants more information or needs clarification on specific words, terms, concepts, places, or people mentioned in the Bible. A Bible dictionary, Bible atlas, concordance, and one-volume Bible commentary together make for a good, basic reference library.

The Leader's Role

An effective leader prepares ahead. This leader guide provides easy-to-follow, step-by-step suggestions for leading a group. The key task of the leader is to guide discussion and activities that will engage heart and head and will invite faith development. Discussion questions are included, and you may want to add questions posed by you or your group. Here are suggestions for helping your group engage Scripture:

State questions clearly and simply.

Ask questions that move Bible truths from "outside" (dealing with concepts, ideas, or information about a passage) to "inside" (relating to the experiences, hopes, and dreams of the participants).

Work for variety in your questions, including compare and contrast, information recall, motivation, connections, speculation, and evaluation.

Avoid questions that call for yes-or-no responses or answers that are obvious.

Don't be afraid of silence during a discussion. It often yields especially thoughtful comments.

Test questions before using them by attempting to answer them yourself.

When leading a discussion, pay attention to the mood of your group by "listening" with your eyes as well as your ears.

Guidelines for the Group

IMMERSION is designed to promote full engagement with the Bible for the purpose of growing faith and building up Christian community. While much can be gained from individual reading, a group Bible study offers an ideal setting in which to achieve these aims. Encourage participants to bring their Bibles and read from Scripture during the session. Invite participants to consider the following guidelines as they participate in the group:

Respect differences of interpretation and understanding.

Support one another with Christian kindness, compassion, and courtesy.

Listen to others with the goal of understanding rather than agreeing or disagreeing.

Celebrate the opportunity to grow in faith through Bible study.

Approach the Bible as a dialogue partner, open to the possibility of being challenged or changed by God's Word.

Recognize that each person brings unique and valuable life experiences to the group and is an important part of the community.

Reflect theologically—that is, be attentive to three basic questions: What does this say about God? What does this say about me/us? What does this say about the relationship between God and me/us?

Commit to a lived faith response in light of insights you gain from the Bible. In other words, what changes in attitudes (how you believe) or actions (how you behave) are called for by God's Word?

Group Sessions

The group sessions, like the chapters themselves, are built around three sections: "Claim Your Story," "Enter the Bible Story," and "Live the Story." Sessions are designed to move participants from an awareness of their own life story, issues, needs, and experiences into an encounter and dialogue with the story of Scripture and to make decisions integrating their personal stories and the Bible's story.

The session plans in the following pages will provide questions and activities to help your group focus on the particular content of each chapter. In addition to questions and activities, the plans will include chapter title, Scripture, and faith focus.

Here are things to keep in mind for all the sessions:

Prepare Ahead

Study the Scripture, comparing different translations and perhaps a paraphrase.

Read the chapter, and consider what it says about your life and the Scripture.

Gather materials such as large sheets of paper or a markerboard with markers.

Prepare the learning area. Write the faith focus for all to see.

Welcome Participants

Invite participants to greet one another.

Tell them to find one or two people and talk about the faith focus.

Ask: What words stand out for you? Why?

Guide the Session

Look together at "Claim Your Story." Ask participants to give their reactions to the stories and examples given in each chapter. Use questions from the session plan to elicit comments based on personal experiences and insights.

Ask participants to open their Bibles and "Enter the Bible Story." For each portion of Scripture, use questions from the session plan to help participants gain insight into the text and relate it to issues in their own lives.

Step through the activity or questions posed in "Live the Story." Encourage participants to embrace what they have learned and to apply it in their daily lives.

Invite participants to offer their responses or insights about the boxed material in "Across the Testaments," "About the Scripture," and "About the Christian Faith."

Close the Session

Encourage participants to read the following week's Scripture and chapter before the next session.

Offer a closing prayer.

1. God Is on Your Side!
Deuteronomy 1–4

Faith Focus

God's generous love invites our grateful and equally generous response.

Before the Session

Get a copy of the lyrics of the hymn "Trust and Obey" from a hymnal, or do a search on the Internet, download the lyrics, and make copies for participants (the lyrics are in the public domain). On a large sheet of paper, print the following questions: How do you know whether someone is trustworthy? How much do you trust God? On another sheet of paper, print and post the words "I consider my land (property) to be . . ." Take time as you begin preparation for this study to consider how you yourself respond to God's generous love. Do you take it for granted, or do you respond with generosity?

Claim Your Story

Invite participants to respond to the first question you posted about how they decide whom to trust. What role does relationship play in developing trust? What does consistency of actions have to do with it? What happens when someone acts in ways that violate our trust? Invite group members to reflect on a time when they destroyed someone's trust in them. What did they do to restore that person's trust in them? Ask volunteers to share aloud an experience they've had.

Ask the group to reflect in silence on the second question about how much they trust God. Note that the study writer tells us that this was the crux of the matter for ancient Israel, as the group will discover in exploring the Book of Deuteronomy.

Enter the Bible Story

The study writer observes that, true to the Hebrew etymology of its name, the Book of Deuteronomy is a book of crucial words. It is a collection of laws and teachings building on the first law, the Ten Commandments.

Deuteronomy repeatedly emphasizes that the land is a gift from God, one that must be claimed by the people. Invite volunteers to read aloud the verses from the book that refer to abundance and to a land filled with milk and honey. What else does God provide (6:10-11)? Also note that the land is closely related to the law.

Invite volunteers to name the four Israels the study writer identifies, and print these four on a large sheet of paper, along with a brief description of each. What is the pattern of continuity that connects these four? In what ways do we ourselves alternate between fear and faith, joyful obedience and stubborn rebellion? What spiritual practices might strengthen our trust in God, so that we might be motivated to more fully obey?

Call the attention of the group to the words "I consider my land (property) to be . . ." and ask them to respond to these words. In our culture and time, how do we view property? Does our view of ownership reflect an understanding that all we claim to possess is really God's gift, or do we view land and other property as our own possessions? In uncertain economic times, how is that understanding shaped by the specter of foreclosures on mortgages? Do we show signs, as did the Israelites, of what the study writer identifies as sloth? What are the fears and anxieties that paralyze us today? How does sloth undermine our hope for the future?

Invite the group to silently read Deuteronomy 1:9-18. What are the four instructions Moses gives to those who would serve as his leadership team? Ask someone to read aloud the quotation from Martin Luther. How does the group respond? Why is calling the powerful to accountability a divine virtue?

Invite someone to read aloud what the study writer refers to as a hidden gem, Deuteronomy 1:30-31. Then designate one side of your meeting space as "warrior/protector image" and the other "parent image." Ask participants to choose the image with which they most resonate and to move to that side of the space and stand there. Urge people reluctant to make this forced choice to decide which one most expresses how they experience God. Invite volunteers to explain why they made the choice they did. What is missing if we view God using just one of these metaphors? How is our experience of God enhanced if we consider both images? How are both images revealed in the verses that rehearse God's history with the people?

Live the Story

Ask participants to reflect on the study writer's affirmation that we can claim the legacy of freedom *from* bondage and freedom *for* a covenantal relationship with God. Then invite them to respond, popcorn style, to the following prompts: "As a Christian, I am freed *from* . . ." and "As a Christian, I am freed *for* . . ." Close by singing together the first stanza and the refrain to the hymn "Trust and Obey."

2. A Relationship and a Way of Living
Deuteronomy 5:1–6:19

Faith Focus

The Ten Commandments and the Great Commandment are the bedrock for living according to God's will.

Before the Session

Set aside ten large sheets of paper. If you like, cut each in the shape of the stone tablets on which the commandments were inscribed. On each sheet, print one of the Ten Commandments. You'll also need ten felt-tipped markers, along with self-stick notes, paper, and pens or pencils.

Claim Your Story

Call the group's attention to the study writer's anecdote about the four young men waiting in line to buy smartphones and to the questions the study writer poses about what symbol one would choose to wear on one's forehead. Distribute self-stick notes and pens or pencils and invite participants to make their own symbols for what they care about most, then stick the notes to their foreheads. Encourage them to be brutally honest with themselves, reflecting on what their day-to-day lives reveal about what they value, and not just to draw a cross or other Christian symbol without some thought. Together, discuss what each person depicted. Do some participants feel they need a different symbol for work, home, church, or other settings as the study writer wonders? If persons in the group were to sketch out a pyramid of what they value, would relationship with God and with others and a way of living be at the top? Would others who interact with them be able to see those values clearly reflected in their lives?

Enter the Bible Story

The study writer observes that, like the Israelites, we who are given these commandments are already God's people—God's love precedes God's commands. Divide the group into ten small groups or pairs of participants and assign one of the Ten Commandments to each. (In a very small group, individuals may need to take on one or more commandments.) Give each group the appropriate "stone tablet" and a felt-tipped marker. Ask them to read the Scripture passage that includes their assigned commandment and the information in the study about this commandment and record what they find about the following questions:

- On its face, what does this commandment mean?
- What information in the study sheds light on its ancient context and deeper meaning?
- In our context, what deeper implications or current applications do you find?
- What questions do you have about how this commandment relates to your life? To our life together as a faith community?

Allow the small groups to work for five minutes or so. Then invite each one to post their tablet and share some of the observations and questions they surfaced with the total group, beginning with the group that considered the first commandment. When every group has reported, invite participants to consider which of the commandments they find most difficult to observe, given what they have just discovered about the fullest sense of each commandment and what it requires. Are there implications about taking God's name in vain, for example, or stealing or killing that they had never considered before? What are the implications of considering the positive side of a commandment?

Invite the group to listen—really listen—as a volunteer reads aloud Deuteronomy 6:4-9, focusing on the word *hear.* What do they hear? How do they respond to the study writer's questions about the import of the two meanings in these verses—that God is neither divided nor capricious? What about the affirmation that God is consistent, always caring and on our side? What does it mean that *freedom from* is always linked to *freedom for?*

Live the Story

Ask a volunteer to read aloud again the Great Commandment, Deuteronomy 6:5. Ask other volunteers to read aloud the commandment as it appears in the New Testament in Matthew 22:34-40, Mark 12:28-34, and Luke 10:25-38. Invite participants to consider again the symbol they created in the opening activity. What does that symbol reveal about their ultimate loyalty? Note that the study writer emphasizes both that we are commanded to love God, demonstrated in the way we live our lives, and that the commandment calls for our total commitment.

Distribute paper and pencils or pens. Invite the group to draw a symbol or print a phrase that represents their commitment to God. They might want to print the Great Commandment in the center of the sheet. Then ask them to print words or draw symbols in a circle around that central commitment that represent the many lesser loves in their lives. In silence, invite them to reflect on how that central commitment is reflected in the ways they live out their commitment to those secondary loyalties and interests. What are ways they might strengthen the way the central commitment reveals itself in their lives?

3. Remembering the Lord's Provisions
Deuteronomy 7–11

Faith Focus

The best motivation for keeping God's commandments is gratitude for the grace God has already shown us.

Before the Session

On a large sheet of paper or a white- or chalkboard, print the following: "I believe I deserve to enjoy the benefits of working hard." Also print Charlie Anderson's blessing on a large sheet of paper. (See "Claim Your Story," page 27.) Again make available copies of the hymn "Trust and Obey," and gather paper and pencils or pens.

Claim Your Story

Call the attention of the group to the statement you posted, and ask group members to respond with a thumbs up or a thumbs down. Invite volunteers to explain why they responded as they did. How much of our personal success can we attribute to our own hard work? In terms of personal experience, where would members of the group place themselves on a continuum from the sharecropper to the wealthy rancher? Are there those in the group who have worked hard and done everything "by the book," yet experienced financial hardship (particularly recently)? How might this experience affect the way persons view how we achieve success? The study writer notes that the material contentment of the later generation of Israelites to whom Deuteronomy is addressed had led to spiritual atrophy and that they needed to hear a message that afflicts the comfortable. What about those of us who are comfortable?

Enter the Bible Story

Invite someone to read aloud Deuteronomy 7:7-11. According to these verses, why did God choose Israel? What does grace have to do with it? The study writer observes that Deuteronomy was written long after the people of Israel moved into the Promised Land, when it was evident that the Israelites did not in fact kill the entire population. They also had a long and checkered history of compromise with pagan values. The study writer sees in this chapter a message that Israel's response to God should mirror God's relationship with Israel. What does obedience have to do with it?

Ask someone to read aloud 1 Peter 2:9. What is it that sets aside Christians as a chosen people? Read aloud the paragraph in the chapter about culture. (See the sidebar "A Holy Nation, God's Own People in the New Testament," page 31.) Invite the group to respond to and discuss the quotation from Thomas Mann. What is it about the way we live our lives that sets us apart from our culture? What evidence can they cite that this particular faith group is living its Christian calling in a manner consistent with the gospel? Where do they see examples of creeping idolatry?

Invite two or three volunteers to read aloud Deuteronomy 8 as the rest of the group listens. Encourage them to visualize the plenty the writer of Deuteronomy is picturing in this speech of Moses. Deuteronomy stresses over and over that Israel finds its true life by remembering what God has done and by keeping the commandments. The context for deciding whether to trust and obey, says the study writer, is specific to each Israel. What is the context in which we must decide? What cultural forces shape that decision? Like the Israelites, are we living in abundance, and therefore inclined toward theological amnesia? Is the test of fullness harder than the test of hunger?

Ask someone to read aloud Deuteronomy 10:12-13. Then have someone read Micah 6:8. What do both of these passages have to say about how we are to live our lives as Christians? What does it mean to circumcise our hearts? How is this connected to doing justice?

Live the Story

Invite the group to discuss the impact of the "attitude of gratitude." Would they agree that the best motivation for keeping God's commandments is thankfulness? Distribute copies of "Trust and Obey" (or post a copy of the refrain). Ask the group to rewrite the refrain to reflect how thankfulness serves as a motivation to trust God and obey God's commandments.

The study writer observes that one way to cultivate a sense of gratitude is to give thanks to God at meals. Call the group's attention to Charlie Anderson's blessing, one that could be called a reflection of a cultural assumption that we alone are responsible for our own well-being. Invite the group to share table graces that reflect gratitude to God as the source for all that we have. Then distribute paper and pens or pencils and invite the group to write prayers that reflect a deeper sense of gratitude, using some of the study writer's suggestions. Invite volunteers to share their prayers with the group. Encourage them to use these prayers in the coming week to further cultivate a sense of gratitude to God for all that God has provided. If table grace is not a practice in their homes, invite them to initiate this ritual, too.

4. Open Heart and Open Hand
Deuteronomy 12:1–16:17

Faith Focus

As people chosen by God, we are called to embody God's concern for the poor and vulnerable.

Before the Session

In the center of a large sheet of paper, print the words, "People Living in Poverty." Draw three concentric circles around the words. Label the one closest to the center "daily interaction"; label the second circle "give money or goods to help"; and label the third "read or see news accounts about." Secure felt-tipped markers. Obtain three large sheets of paper and label each with the name of one of the three great pilgrimage festivals: Passover; Weeks (Pentecost; Shavu'ot); and Booths (Sukkot). Do an Internet search for additional information about these Jewish festivals. One good source is www.jewfaq.org. Download and print any information you think will add to the group's discussion. Check with your pastor to see what programs, both local and national in scope, your denomination has to address poverty, and what local agencies and initiatives participants might be a part of.

Claim Your Story

As participants arrive, invite them to print their name in the circle on the large sheet of paper that represents the most direct contact they have with people who are living in poverty. Ask volunteers to describe their interaction: Do they live in a neighborhood with people of limited income, and do they personally know people who are poor? Do their children attend school with children who are poor? Are they involved in work such as social work with people who are poor? Do they regularly give money or goods to programs that address poverty? Is their primary or only contact reading or seeing news accounts about poverty? Is poverty an issue about which they care deeply and which they seek to address, or something that really does not touch their day-to-day lives? What is the connection between their faith and ministry with people who are poor?

Enter the Bible Story

Call the group's attention to the information in the chapter about apostasy and idolatry. The study writer reminds us that Deuteronomy's audience was the people of Israel living after the collapse of Jerusalem and Judah. The writing is concerned with how the disasters the people had endured could have been avoided. Remind the group of the exercise in the second session about where we place our priorities—those things or practices that become our idols. How have these "idols" contributed to making vulnerable people, especially children, more vulnerable? Are we guilty of sacrificing our children or the children of others to a pursuit of material gain, for example?

The study writer observes that when Israel inherits the land, God emerges as the protector of those individuals and groups who are landless. Some means of breaking the cycle of poverty were necessary in that time. What about in ours? Invite participants to pair up. Ask one person in each pair to read the Scripture and information in the chapter about the sabbatical year (including forgiveness of debts: pages 40-41), and the other about release from debt-slavery (page 41). Each pair should share information about their assigned topic. Tell the group that these measures were designed to break the cycle of poverty and dependence. What about today? What measures can Christians support to address systemic poverty and deprivation?

Invite someone to read aloud Deuteronomy 15:7-11; then ask other volunteers to read aloud Matthew 26:11, Mark 14: 7, and John 12: 8. The study writer observes that although there are those who use these words of Jesus to rationalize doing nothing about poverty, Jesus was actually referring to Deuteronomy. How does this reference turn indifference to poor people on its ear?

Designate part of your space for each of the three pilgrimage festivals (Passover, Weeks, Booths). Ask participants to select one of the festivals. Then ask participants within each of these small groups to read the Scripture and study text about their festival, as well as any other information you make available. Ask them to generate three or four questions about the festival for the rest of the group to answer. Reassemble the total group and involve participants in discussing the questions each small group generated. What connections does the group find to remembering? To gratitude? Who was included?

Live the Story

Invite the group to brainstorm ways your congregation, and they as individuals, are already involved in addressing poverty and ways they might be engaged. Using the categories the study writer enumerates, list suggested ideas on large sheets of paper or on a white- or chalkboard. When the brainstorming seems to have run its course, invite participants to read over the ideas in silence. Then enter into a time of prayer, asking God for discernment for where God is calling each person to engage in discipleship. Name each category of action in turn and allow a time of silent prayer. Then close by reading "Christ Has No Body" (page 45).

5. Grand Central Story
Deuteronomy 6:20-25; 16:18–26:15

Faith Focus

We know who God is and who we are when we claim for ourselves the historical story of the people of God.

Before the Session

Down the left margin of a large sheet of paper, list the following: The Declaration of Independence; Lincoln's Gettysburg Address; The Women's Suffrage Movement; Martin Luther King, Jr.'s "I Have a Dream" speech. Leave a fair amount of space between these four events that the study writer identifies as elements of the larger American story. Provide paper and pens or pencils for participants. From a hymnal or the Internet, obtain the lyrics to the hymn "I Love to Tell the Story" and make copies for participants. Also make copies of the Apostles' Creed, enough for each participant to have a copy.

Claim Your Story

Call the group's attention to the four elements of the American story. Are there other stories they would name that also are key elements of our central American story? If so, list these in the appropriate chronological place on the sheet. Can they name other "midcourse corrections" to the story? What other aspects of the American story are embodied in our common story as a people? Are there subtexts that certain groups would claim as central that others would not acknowledge? What parts of our story say, "This is who we are. This is how we act"? What parts delineate who we are *not*? In our common life as people of faith—people of God—what is the role of retelling our story?

Enter the Bible Story

Invite participants to give some thought to some event or narrative from their own lives that seems to them to be what Thomas Mann would call their grand central story—the organizing story for all the stories of their lives. Invite volunteers to briefly share such a story and to tell how it has shaped them. How has it influenced what they did or did not do?

Review the five points the study writer lifts up from the passage identified as Israel's grand central story, Deuteronomy 26:5-10. Then urge the group to listen for these five aspects as someone reads the passage aloud. To which of these five aspects can participants relate? Which aspects seem more remote? Does the telling and retelling of narratives from the Bible provide a bridge and a bond between these ancient people and us? How is this story our story, too? Ask another volunteer to read Deuteronomy 6:20-25, another summary of Israel's grand central story. The study writer observes that the law is a part of that story. Does the law provide boundaries for us, too? How does it define who we are?

Maintenance of justice, says the study writer, was a core value of the covenant community, and denial of justice was an offense comparable to idolatry. Ask participants to name ancient legal traditions and duties cited by the study writer that were intended to extend justice to the most vulnerable. Are there parallels between these requirements in the Torah and services a government might provide to those who are trapped in the web of poverty? As Christians, how do we make provision for justice for these vulnerable ones? Can the church take care of all the needs of those living in poverty, or is there a need for systemic change and policies to provide for them?

The study writer poses the question as to the relevance of Deuteronomy's criteria for leadership to our twenty-first-century context. In the light of the discussion in the study, invite the group to consider what would be the positive virtues for someone in a leadership role in our government, such as an elected office. Ask participants to form small groups of three or four and to make a list of qualities they would find desirable in a candidate for such a position, and then to write a political ad for a fictitious candidate that emphasizes these qualities. Reassemble the total group and share these ads.

Live the Story

Ask participants to briefly summarize Christianity's grand central story. How is it grafted onto Israel's story in the Old Testament? Which New Testament narratives can they name that best illumine the story for them? Invite the group to reflect on the first question posed by the study writer in the last paragraph of the study (page 55). Generate a list of the practices in which your congregation engages and the commitments it has made to claim and embody the Christian story. Point out that the study writer notes that every time we recite the Apostles'

Creed we retell the story. Distribute copies of the Apostles' Creed and invite the group to recite it together. Encourage the group to consider in the coming week the final three questions the study writer lists and to reflect on their responses.

Close by singing "I Love to Tell the Story" together.

6. Choose Life!
Deuteronomy 26:16–34:12

Faith Focus
God calls us to live faithfully each and every day.

Before the Session
On a large sheet of paper, print the following: "Now is the time for all good persons to . . ." Obtain a basin and place in it some small smooth glass stones (available from a craft store). Also obtain a pitcher of water to use in the reaffirmation of baptism at the conclusion of this study. Cut sheets of paper in irregular "rock" shapes and plan to build an "altar" on a large sheet of paper. Head two separate large sheets of paper with the following: "Blessings for Obedience" and "Warnings Against Disobedience."

Claim Your Story
Invite participants to name important commitments they have made. Discuss the questions posed by the study writer about honoring commitments and keeping promises. Talk about what happens when we fail in doing this. One writer observes that since we are all sinners and will inevitably fall short, it is not so much the failure to keep promises, but rather the failure to keep making promises anew, that cuts us off from relationship.[1] Ask the group to respond to this idea. Explain that you will consider what Deuteronomy has to say about the most important choices we make.

Enter the Bible Story
Invite participants to complete the prompt you posted. Some may remember how that sentence was competed in typing class: ". . . to come to the aid of their country." What in their lives holds the urgency that requires a response *now*? In Deuteronomy, the demands God makes of one generation are made of every generation, and that continuity is expressed in urgent terms. Invite volunteers to read the verses in the chapter that reflect events as contemporaneous. Encourage the group to name events in their lives that seem in the retelling as vivid as if they were actually happening in the present.

The inclusiveness of the covenant extends across social distinctions. Does your congregation include a broad social and class spectrum? What, if anything, is the value of learning to be disciples in an intergenerational, multiclass, multicultural environment?

Divide the group into two smaller groups. Assign to one Deuteronomy 28:1-6 and to the other, Deuteronomy 28:15-19. Though the remainder of the verses in chapter 28 contain much more exhaustive admonitions about blessings and curses, ask the two groups to read over the assigned verses, make comparable contemporary lists of blessings and curses ("Blessed shall you be . . ." "Cursed shall you be . . .") and then print them on the appropriate sheets of paper. Ask the groups to read aloud the completed lists. What reaction does the total group have to the idea that bounty and deprivation are linked to obedience or disobedience? What about the idea that natural disasters happen as a direct result of people's disobedient behavior? The study writer observes that when an entire society is wrong, the consequences can be devastating for generations. Does the group agree or disagree? Racism and environmental degradation are two examples to illustrate this idea. Can participants think of others? If curse is not the final word and blessing and obedience are still possible, how does this happen? How do the ideas of justification and sanctification play into this? Would the group agree that grace and response must be simultaneous, as the study writer suggests?

In times of change when a leader must be replaced, confidence and trust in God's presence is key. Invite the group to quickly scan Deuteronomy 31:30–32:47. In addition to the images of God the group considered in an earlier session (warrior and parent), this passage includes two more: rock and eagle. What does each of these four metaphors tell us about God? Which ones are the most telling for participants, and why? How do these descriptors increase our understanding of God, and perhaps our trust?

Live the Story

Call participants' attention to the illustration of what it means to give our all to God "25 cents" at a time. Reflect on the question of what we are doing to choose life, keeping in mind that most of us do this a quarter at a time. Distribute the paper "rocks" you prepared, and invite each person to print 25 cents' worth of what they are doing to choose life—one of the small day-to-day choices they make. Attach the rocks to the prepared surface in the shape of an altar.

As Christians we choose life through baptism. Ask the group to sit in silence reflecting on how, in the waters of baptism, God chooses us. Pour the water into the basin and invite each person to dip a hand in the water, remembering his or her baptism and taking a glass stone as a reminder.

1. Craig Dykstra, *Growing in the Life of Faith: Education and Christian Practices*, second edition (Westminster John Knox Press, 2005); see pages 100-101.

93